RAPED

RAPED

Deborah Roberts

ZONDERVAN
PUBLISHING HOUSE
OF THE ZONDERVAN CORPORATION
GRAND RAPIDS, MICHIGAN 49506

Library of Congress Cataloging in
Publication Data
Roberts, Deborah.
　Raped.
　　1. Roberts, Deborah. 2. Rape victims
— United States — Biography. I. Title.
HV6561.R6A37　362.8'8　[B] 81-11408
ISBN 0-310-43680-X　　　AACR2

"Into Your Hands" by Ray Repp (refrain
adapted to first-person singular) is used by
permission of F.E.L. Publications, Ltd.,
Los Angeles, California.

Designed and edited by Judith E. Markham

Printed in the United States of America

to my husband

The names and places have been changed in this otherwise true account to protect the privacy of the individuals involved.

An appendix has been added to provide additional information concerning the crime of rape.

To Dave

You believed in this project from its inception. Like no one else could, you walked every step of the road with me, offering never-ending support and self-sacrifice. You willingly became a sounding board, providing exceptional aid, especially in the final stages. You faced painful moments with strength, never allowing the thought of quitting to enter your mind or mine. For all this book has required of you and will require of you in the days ahead, I am deeply grateful.

To Rev. Jennings

Many of the pages of this book should be initialed by you. You provided guidance and insight which contributed to both the seasoning and the substance of this book. You took countless risks in challenging me and made yourself available whenever I needed your feedback or encouragement. But more than this, by helping me to face even the darkest corners of my life with confidence, you have helped me to grow yet another set of wings. For all you have given, thank you.

I am more than unusually grateful to the people at the Zondervan Corporation for their warmth and enthusiasm and for having the courage to publish this book. I am particularly indebted to my editor, Judith Markham, who challenged me with sensitivity and understanding, and gave me freedom beyond the bounds of comfort. I also wish to express my appreciation to Jan, who has been invaluable both as a hard-working typist and a caring friend; to LeRoy, who read my manuscript and encouraged me to seek its publication; to my fellow rape crisis team members, who provided me with new insight into the crime of rape, with special thanks to Faye;

to the victims who shared their experiences with me; to Bev, Pat B., and Pat H., friends who lovingly took care of our children so I could work on the book; to Tom, who provided the use of his office and frequent encouragement; to Joyce, Glenn, and Phyllis, who gave me space and never asked questions; to Paul's mom and dad, who spent their day with us in the neighborhood ten years later; to Beth and Jeremy, who patiently waited for me to complete this project; and to my friends and relatives who offered their prayers and continually asked, "How's the book going?" To all of you, no matter how large or seemingly small a part you played, please accept my deepest gratitude.

Introduction

My friend's son had drowned only two days before. He was beautiful. He was vivacious. He was five years old.

As I waited to offer Laurie whatever support I could, I overheard the woman ahead of me say, "Laurie, you know that I know what you're going through." Tears were streaming down her cheeks as she continued, "It was a long time ago, but—"

Laurie completed her statement, "But it comes back hard, doesn't it?" The woman broke down and could not control the flow of tears.

I didn't know this other woman or her situation, but I understood from the conversation that she must have experienced the loss of a loved one, maybe even a child of her own, some years before. She was only trying to help, trying to share in Laurie's grief; instead, her message was that many years later, she still hurt terribly.

I know the pain that comes with the death of a loved one, especially your own child, and the pain of rape are not to be compared. They are two completely different hurts. Yet something about this incident spoke to me. It has to do with the message I mean to give to you, the reader.

Though my honesty and forthrightness often get me into trouble, here I feel it is necessary to tell the whole truth, omitting nothing, not even the sexual adjustment to rape. Rape is horrible, and I must show openly how horrible an experience it is.

But I cannot stop there. You see, the message of this book is the message I wish that woman had been able to convey to my friend, Laurie: *Our God is a big God.* And there is no tragedy so great that each of us, together with God, cannot get through. If we hold onto His promises, we can reach a day when the pain no longer rages and the tears no longer flow.

But even more than that, for those who love God there is healing. There is wholeness. And there is even joy. There is peace. For in the rebuilding of our lives we discover the fullness of God's love.

1

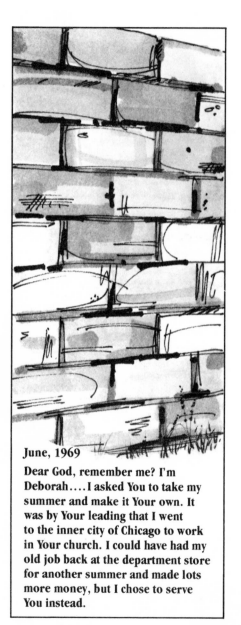

June, 1969

Dear God, remember me? I'm
Deborah....I asked You to take my
summer and make it Your own. It
was by Your leading that I went
to the inner city of Chicago to work
in Your church. I could have had my
old job back at the department store
for another summer and made lots
more money, but I chose to serve
You instead.

As our two-year-old 1967 cranberry Cougar crossed the bridge into the inner-city neighborhood where I would spend my summer, I wondered if our car would make us look like the outsiders we were. I imagined that the people whose lives were so heavily supported by government funds would be driving junkers. Apparently I was wrong. Big black Buicks. Stylish Thunderbirds with the brand-new sequential taillights. How could these people afford such cars? Maybe this neighborhood wasn't so bad after all.

In my narrow mind I had pictured the inner-city living conditions as much worse. I remembered driving past the slums on the south side of Chicago before the Robert Taylor Homes had been built there by the government. Tall, narrow buildings, each a twin to its neighbor, with only a crack of light separating them. From the back there was nothing to view but stairs and banisters . . . five stories of laundry hanging from pulley clotheslines . . . tricycles on six-foot by three-foot porches. Row after row of identical houses with only an occasional tree to break up the cement, the brick, the frame—the hard surfaces that so adequately symbolized the hardness of the residents' lives.

It was years ago that I, as a young child, had seen those slums, but ever since, that was how I had pictured inner-city neighborhoods. Now I had grown and changed. So had the city.

I snapped back to reality and tried to take in all my surroundings. My immediate impression was that it wasn't so bad. The area didn't look too rough. As we turned the corner onto Barclay Street, I could see more of the projects, three-story brick buildings with windows that opened out. They looked institutional but not run-down, at least not from the outside. We turned another corner, stopping on Griswold Street. My father parked in the only space left on the street.

There it was! 1802. The second house from the corner. I was the first one out of the car. My mother, father, and younger sister followed.

The three boys walking toward us on the sidewalk couldn't have been more than nine years old, yet there was something about them that made me uncomfortable. Something was missing . . . a skateboard, a baseball glove, a swimming suit rolled up in a towel . . . they carried nothing. Their walk was a worldly-wise saunter, as if their childhood had already been spent. I wondered if our hubcaps would be there when we returned.

Suddenly I was anxious to see a familiar face in this place. As we approached Reverend Quillan's house, I became aware of a churning in my stomach. My excitement had turned to nervousness. Would I do a good job here? What would my roommate be like? What would this job be like? What would I be doing while I was here? What did the people in my comfortable suburb mean when they said, "It will be a good experience for you. . . . You'll see what the world is really like"? Added to my nervousness was impatience. I wanted to experience it all at once.

There was a bright yellow smiley-face sign above Reverend Quillan's door that read, "Smile, God loves you." It made me feel better, but not comfortable. I would like it here. I knew I would. God had led me here for the summer. It couldn't be any other way.

It had been only two months since I had decided to do something more meaningful than clerk in a department store for another summer. On my college campus was a small meditation chapel that had become a haven for me—a place for peace and quiet and prayer. I had gone there one afternoon to ask God to use my summer for His service. On my way back to the dorm, I had picked up the college bulletin and an ad had caught my eye:

NEEDED

2 college students to work in urban church for 10 weeks this summer. Applications available in chaplain's office.

I hadn't expected God's answer quite so immediately, but responding to an overwhelming, compelling feeling, I went directly to the chaplain's office. I filled out the forms and waited to be called, all the while praying that, if it was within God's will, I might be chosen.

Reverend Quillan, the minister at the inner-city church, came to campus and interviewed twenty-five students, myself included. It all happened so fast that I was chosen before I had even told my parents I had applied for the job.

Deanna was to be my roommate for the summer. Although we both attended the same college, we had not met. It would be fun getting to know Deanna as we worked together. We were going to share Jesus with the people in the city. It would be a wonderful summer. I had seen the faces of those who had accepted Jesus into their lives before. I couldn't wait to see that again. The people there needed Him so much. It would be a wonderful summer. I just knew it!

The entrance to our attic apartment was in the back of the tall, narrow, red brick house where Reverend Quillan and his family lived. Deanna and I had to climb five flights of wooden stairs to reach the top of the three-story building. The first door led into the rough, unfinished outer attic. The second opened into our kitchen where we had an old chrome table, a small refrigerator, and a hot plate. Since we had no plumbing in the kitchen, we washed our dishes in the large footed bathtub and rinsed them in the bathroom sink. We managed without kitchen cupboards, too, keeping everything from tomato soup to laundry detergent on three rows of shelves in a closet we called our pantry.

Our two single beds barely fit under the slant of the roof in the bedroom. A narrow aisle between them allowed us to get to the table with the old black telephone on it or to the window.

Looking out the large window was like sitting on top of the city street. A small tree only partially blocked the view of the concrete below. We could watch the shifts change at strange hours of the day and night at the laundry across the street. It was the first time I had seen people going to work in T-shirts and cutoff jeans. My father had always worn a suit, a tie, and a freshly.pressed shirt to his teaching job. My mother, also a teacher, dressed smartly and tastefully in dresses or skirts and blouses. Here, dirty and sweaty men and women came out of the prisonlike, block-long brick building. I was never aware of a parking lot for the laundry. Probably because most of the people were from the neighborhood. They walked to and from their jobs each day, carrying their black lunch boxes or brown paper sacks.

Usually at the end of a shift a small group of men would gather on the concrete outside the building. They would pause for a cigarette, carrying on loud conversations before heading to their various apartments or row houses. But most of the people who left were women dressed in work shirts and pants. I wondered where their children were while they worked long hours at their factory jobs. We discovered later that many of them were left to fend for themselves. Tommy was one of these children, and I remember vividly the day we met him.

Deanna and I had been out recruiting door-to-door for the Head Start program. We had climbed to the third floor of one of the apartment buildings, and it was my turn to knock on the door. I could hear a TV inside but no one answered the door. I knocked harder. The door pushed open ever so slowly, only a crack. Two puppylike brown eyes, nearly covered by long black curls, peered out at us. At first I couldn't tell if it was a boy or a girl.

"Hello there. I'm Debbie and this is Deanna. What's your name?"

No answer.

"Is your mother home?"

Still no answer.

I turned to Deanna. "Maybe he doesn't speak English."

"Habla Español?"

He just stared. The longer he stared, the more frustrated I became.

"That's okay. Thank you anyway."

"Let's try this door," Deanna suggested, pointing to the apartment just across the hall. An elderly lady answered my knock.

"Hi. We're recruiting for Head Start. We're looking for four- and five-year-olds. Do you know if there are any living in this building? We haven't been able to find anybody at home."

"Uh, don't know. Don't know the folks here."

"Do you happen to know the people across the hall?"

"Some."

"Is there more than one child living there?"

"Nope. Jest Tommy."

"Do you know how old Tommy is?"

"He's eight. But his mom's not here. She's in the hospital. Goin' on two weeks now."

"Oh, I see. What about his father?"

"Never can tell where he's at. Ain't been seen in six months."

"Tommy's all by himself now, then?"

"Yeah, but I look after him when I can."

"Oh, that's very nice of you. Let's see . . . if he's eight, he must be in second or third grade, then?"

"Oh, no. Tommy don't go to school. His mom don't send him."

"Oh, I don't mean in the summer—"

"No. He ain't never been."

"He's never been to school?"

"That's right. His mom don't send him, and the school's never got him. Prob'ly don't know he's here."

"Could you please tell me Tommy's last name?"

"Pierce."

"Thank you. You've been very helpful."

I couldn't believe it! An eight-year-old who had never been to school . . . and living all alone! We would give his name to Reverend Quillan. He would find a way to help Tommy.

Door-to-door recruiting for Head Start and Project Friendly Town taught us a lot about the people in the projects. We were five miles from Lake Michigan, yet many of the kids had never been to the beach. Much of their life was broken glass and asphalt playgrounds.

Even though LSD was available to anyone who wanted it, alcoholism was a bigger problem than drugs. Nearly all the teen-agers drank beer and were usually drunk on the weekends. I wasn't used to that. My family didn't drink at all, and the suburban teen-agers I knew who drank were usually discreet about it. Here everything was out in the open—right on the street!

One afternoon when Deanna and I were talking with some of the kids in the courtyard of an apartment building, a guy came up to me and said, "Want a sip of my beer?"

"No thanks."

"Whatsa matter? Somethin' wrong wit' my beer?"

"Nope. I just don't drink beer."

"You don't drink beer?" He grabbed me by the arm. "Have a sip or I'll pour it over your head."

I just looked up at him and laughed, "Go ahead. I hear beer shampoos are great for your hair!"

Fortunately, for my sake, he decided not to do it. Laughing about it had eased the tension. But the whole drinking problem continued to bother me for the duration of my stay in the city.

One of our objectives for the summer was to organize activities to keep the kids off the streets and out of trouble. Our storefront coffeehouse helped to serve that purpose. The kids could come there several nights a week and play cards, listen to their own kind of music, drink soda pop, and just get together for a good time without the drugs, the beer, or the cops breathing down their necks. On the street they could be arrested for gathering in groups of more than five. At the coffeehouse they could freely mix and share their lives with each other and with us. We got to know a few of them quite well. Rudy is one I will never forget.

"I ain't never been in no po-lice station," he would boast.

"Aw, Rudy, you have so. Everybody been one time 'er 'nother."

"I ain't neither."

"You never been down fer nothin'? You lie, guy. I knows you lie."

"All right. All right, man. I been there. Ta register ma bike, man. But I ain't been there no time else."

The other kids would jeer and give him a hard time, but they respected Rudy more than any other kid on the streets. He was level-headed and somehow managed to keep out of trouble. Because he was such a good influence on the others, he was a big help to us in the coffeehouse.

We hoped to attract Rudy and some of the other teen-agers to come on Sundays as well, when our storefront coffeehouse became our place of worship. On a good Sunday we would have twenty-five to thirty people there. Coming from a suburban church of four hundred families, that didn't seem like much of a church to me at first. But I quickly learned that even though the numbers were few, God was working and changing lives. Ever so slowly, growth was taking place. I acquired a great deal of respect for Reverend Quillan for sticking by those people the four years he had already been there. Rev, as he was affectionately known, was a family man, the father of three young children. He was a simple man, though not in the least ordinary. He held a strong vision for the future of his church. Watching the people in the neighborhood struggle through their daily lives, he worked to bring them meaning and hope through the message of Christ. It was a dream we all shared for the people in the projects. Yet it was a goal that would not be quickly or easily realized.

2

July 5, 1969

I was doing God's work. Nothing could happen to me. Not me. Not there. Not then. Not ever. God would take care of me.

Deanna and I spent the first four weeks in the city recruiting for Project Head Start and Project Friendly Town, tutoring at the Boys' Club, making plans for a backyard school, participating in Sunday worship, helping to run the coffeehouse, and in general trying to get to know the neighborhood and the people in it.

Our fifth week was spent away from the city as counselors at our denomination's church camp. Sometime later in the summer some of the kids from the projects would spend a week at this camp, but this time just Deanna and I went.

We were given two different cabins for the week. All ten of the girls in my cabin were in junior high school, which, I discovered, was a very obnoxious age. But in six short days I grew to love each one of them dearly. On the last day of camp I felt as if I was leaving my own family. I was. Every single one of them had made a personal commitment to Christ the night before. We were family.

And yet I was anxious to get back to my job in the city. After all, that was what this summer was all about. Rev had sent the two of us to camp only because there had been a shortage of counselors for that particular week. My real job was in the projects, and I was ready to return.

Deanna looked tired the morning we left. Even at the young age of nineteen, five or six hours of sleep a night had not been nearly enough for either of us. Since the night before had been the Fourth of July as well as the last night at camp, we had all been up until the "wee hours" laughing, singing, and celebrating in true holiday spirit.

It wasn't until the tearful good-bys had been said and all the campers had gone that Rev arrived to pick us up in the church van. The ride back to the city was long, and by the time we got to our apartment, the week's activities had caught up with us. Exhaustion hit. At 11:30 in the morning Deanna and I were ready for a good night's sleep, but a nap would have to do.

After we had been asleep nearly four-and-a-half hours, the alarm buzzed. Groggy and barely functioning, I managed to find the ten-minute delay button. I slammed my palm down on top of it, silencing the annoying sound. When it rang the second time, I was awake enough to remember that we were back in the city and had work to do. Besides, I was hungry—reason enough to get up.

Deanna was still sound asleep.

"Deanna."

No reply.

"Deanna, get up."

"Huh?"

"Get up. We have to go shopping."

"Shopping? Oh, yeah. Right. Shopping? What for?"

Since we had been gone for a week, we had no food in the apartment. It was a short walk to the neighborhood grocery store, and on our way back we began to plan the week ahead of us. Only one thing had to be taken care of yet that day. Rev had prepared some fliers to inform the people in the projects that the church was moving to the Boys' Club a block away. The storefront we had been renting was to be demolished to make room for a parking lot. The move was only temporary until we could locate another place for the church and the coffeehouse ministry, but since it was to go into effect the next day, we had to get word to the people right away.

Delivering the notices would only take an hour or so, but as Deanna and I set out for the projects, we were both aware that it was quickly becoming Saturday night on the streets of Chicago. It was chilly for the first week in July. I had put on my long blue jeans, a sweatshirt, and my college windbreaker.

The small children were still out, and it was not dark yet,

but it soon would be. If we stayed together, we would not get finished until after dark, so we decided to split up. I took the row houses on the left side of Griswold Street, and Deanna took the three-story apartments on the right side of the street. After I finished on my side, I would cross over and start working my way back until we met. We would be finished in no time.

After I had put the notices in several mailboxes, I stopped on the sidewalk to look back. I didn't see Deanna at first, but in a few seconds she appeared. She waved. Apparently she had been watching for me, too. I waved back. After that I picked up the pace. I would show her how fast I could get my part of the job done.

Feeling confident and in good spirits, I chatted with some of the children along the way. When I came to the end of the street, I noticed a group of guys loitering on the corner, four or five of them. I hadn't seen Deanna for a while and an uneasiness set in, but not enough to squelch my enthusiasm. When I got to the last row house, I realized that they were standing in front of the mailbox. I didn't recognize any of them, but I didn't want to insult them by not going to their house. They had all turned and were staring at me, probably wondering what I was handing out.

I had to pass so close to them that I felt I had to say something, especially since they were all staring at me. So I said, "Hi!" and handed a flier to the nearest one. He grabbed my arm and said, "Want to come to my party?" I could smell the beer on his breath. I pulled my arm back with a curt, "No thank you," crossed the street, and entered the door of the first apartment building.

I heard something behind me. Someone had followed me into the entranceway of the apartment building. It was the one who had grabbed my arm, and he was between me and the door I had just come through . . . the only way out. It was only five feet away but out of reach. I put the notices into the mailboxes with a rhythm that matched the rapid tempo of my heartbeat, then turned to leave as quickly as possible.

"Where you goin'?"

"I'm leaving. I'm all done here. Excuse me." I tried to move past him, but he pushed me up against the wall.

"How about goin' to my party, huh?"

"Sorry. I've got work to do." Funny. There had been several guys standing outside, but no girls. I hadn't heard any music . . . no real signs of a party. What did he want?

The answer to this question came suddenly. He threw me up against the wall a second time and stuck his dirty hands up inside my sweatshirt. He grabbed my bra, yanking it up. At the instant his hands touched my breasts, I shrunk from the inside out and struggled to get past him to the door. I made it to the door and could have made it out if I could have just pushed the door open, but the door had to be opened toward me, and he was right there behind me.

He pushed me around and put himself between me and my only escape route. I knew I was in trouble. Where was Deanna? If I could just stall him. She would be coming soon. He reached for his back pocket and threatened, "Now I don't want to hurt you." I knew he had a knife there. Everyone on these streets carried knives. I could see him clearly now. He had a pockmarked complexion and short, fuzzy hair. But it was the look in his eyes that frightened me most. I had never seen such a repulsive, wicked expression of desire and power.

I had no doubts now. I knew what he was after.

"Would it matter to you if I told you I had syphillis? I do, you know." Anything to stall him.

"Who's your boyfriend?"

Maybe this was my chance. "He's a Black Spider." I knew

the Black Spiders were a gang from outside the neighborhood. Was that enough to scare him off?

"Does he know Joe?"

"Of course." *Who's Joe?* How long could I carry this bluff? Had I already blown it? *Dear Lord, help me.*

He unzipped my jeans. "I'm having my period," I pleaded. It didn't seem to matter to him.

I had inched away from the wall. He threw me up against it again. And again I tried to get away, but couldn't get past him. I could fake fainting. It wouldn't be too tough to fake. I was beginning to feel very weak as it was. *Dear Lord, help me faint. Get me out of this, please God.* My body became totally limp, and I slumped to the floor. *No! O God! No! Make him leave me alone!* He had picked up my feet and was dragging me away, away from the door, away from the street, down the stairs that led to the basement. *O God, who can help me now?* I prayed again. *Lord, please spare me this. Let me live. . . . I know. He thinks I've passed out. When he lets go of my legs, I'll jump up and startle him enough to break away and make a run for it.*

As my foot hit the second step, I felt the burn of captivity singe through my arm, then through my entire body. He had ahold of me. He reached for his blade again. "I don't want to hurt you," he said, not with compassion, but with a life-threatening sting. He wrenched my hand from the banister, shoving me to the basement floor. Where was Deanna? *What if she doesn't find me down here? What if she goes home without me?*

The floor was filthy. I could feel it all around me. The stench of urine permeated the air.

"Take off your pants."

I couldn't move.

He pulled off one leg of my jeans . . . then my underpants. I couldn't watch. I could hear him loosen his belt and remove his pants. He pushed my feet up so that my knees were in the air.

That moment . . . that single moment of pain. No, the word "pain" cannot touch it. There is no word to describe it. It cannot be compared to a burn or a gunshot wound or a broken bone or a knife piercing the body. It's a pain like no other. It's a pain that kills. It kills every breath of life within. All energy . . . all will to resist . . . gone . . . dead. Defeated. *I can't move. I'm not me. I'm not here. I am dead. I am nothing. I am . . . no longer.*

That moment in time . . . no, there was no moment. There was no time. There was nothing but evil. *My God, where are you? My God, my God. Where are you? Evil crushes me. Grinds me into dust. Oh, my God. I can't bear it. I can't bear it. Why have you left me? Oh, God, where are you? Help me. Someone. Please help me. . . .*

"You're a virgin," he mocked.

"Yes." A whisper was all I could get out.

The sound of the door opening startled me. Someone was at the top of the stairs, only a few steps away. His hand smothered my mouth. I thought he would break my jaw. *Oh, my God . . . I don't want anyone to see me like this. Please, God, let this person help, but don't let anyone see.*

"Debbie, are you down there?" Thank God. It was Deanna.

He fumbled for his back pocket again. Before he released my mouth, he whispered intensely with his face inches from mine, "Get rid of her. I know where you live."

"Yeah, Deanna . . . go . . . on ahead."

There was a pause. Then the sound of the door opening and . . . closing. She had left. With her went what particle of strength I had left. What was I to do now?

A few minutes passed as he continued thrusting himself into me. The door opened again.

"Debbie?"

"Deanna?"

"Get rid of her or I'll get her, too!" he hissed.

What could I say to alert her without angering him into killing me? *Lord, help.*

"Should I go back to the place?" she asked before I could think of anything to say to her.

"Yes, I think that would be a good idea." *Oh, Lord. What place?* What did she mean? Did she sense my danger? Was she going to get Rev or was she just going home? I had to believe she was going for help. I had to.

Even after those interruptions, he kept forcing himself into me. Then he stopped.

"I'm taking you back to my party." Terror struck. No! His friends! They'll get me too! No! If we left, Deanna would never find me. There were hundreds of apartments on this block. I had to stall. He stood up, pulling his pants on.

"Get up!" He seemed nervous now and kept looking toward the top of the stairs. Pulling up his zipper, he yelled at me again. "Hurry up! You're going to my party."

I sat up very slowly, delaying as much as I dared. Before my clothes were fully adjusted, he grabbed my arm and dragged me behind him up the stairs. I knew I had to try to break loose when we got on the street. It was my only chance.

"Don't forget, we all know where you live," he threatened again as we reached the entryway. Just then the door opened. It was Rev. I felt a surge of relief and a new fear all at the same time. What if his friends were still out there? What if they hurt Rev, too? They could kill us both!

I deliberately fastened my belt so that Rev could see, hoping that would reveal to him what had happened.

"What were you doing down there?" Rev demanded. The magnitude of his voice did not match the small, almost frail frame of his body. Rev was street tough, even though his build did not reflect that fact.

Somehow my captor managed to scream in my ear at a whisper's pitch, "I want him to see you kiss me. Tell him you're my girl friend or I'll get you. My friends know where to find you." He was reaching for his knife again.

When we got out on the street, I could see the church van. Deanna was in it. It was an object of safety, and I was not far from it. Would this horrid ordeal finally end? The other guys were not in sight, but they could be anywhere . . . watching. I was positive they were.

He still gripped my arm tightly. "I gotta talk ta my girl," he said to Rev, pulling me a few feet away so that we were still in plain sight, but out of normal voice range. Rev watched intently, looking angry but confused.

"Do it. Kiss me. Now." His mouth attacked mine and I felt my lips being forced open by his tongue. Repulsed by this vulgar act, I wanted to back away. But he had his arms strapped tight to my back and I was captive still. "Show the Rev this was all your idea," he insisted. Afraid of what he might do if I didn't, I put my arms around him. In front of Rev, in front of Deanna, in front of the whole world. Although I was clothed, I was naked and all could see.

He stopped only long enough to threaten me again. "Don't you call the pigs, you hear?" He crammed the words into my ear as he tightened his grip.

"Again, baby." He forced his awful kiss on me again.

Rev walked toward us. "Let go of her. Debbie, get in the van." Rev was taking control of the situation.

I felt his grip loosen . . . I was released.

"Are you all right?" Rev asked gently as I walked by him.

I nodded. I could not find words to break through the wall of my humiliation. As I reached the van, I could hear Rev asking his name. "Joe Namath," was the reply.

I watched from the van as the two of them stood face to face. The guy kept reaching for his back pocket, and I knew he was threatening Rev too. I searched the street outside the van with my eyes and ears, fearful that his friends were still around. Deanna tried to start up a conversation. "I've never seen him before . . . what are they talking about?" she asked. I couldn't respond. I was terrified for Rev.

A moment later Rev was walking back to the van, and the attacker headed across the street to the row house where I had first seen him. He ducked around the building and was gone. It was over. We were all safe. I pulled air into my lungs and let it out again. It hurt. My entire body ached.

As Rev climbed into the van, Deanna turned toward me and asked, "Do you want to go to the clinic?"

Did she know what had happened in there? Did Rev? They must. I was relieved. It meant I didn't have to tell them.

As we were sitting there in the van, a police car drove up and parked behind us. Two policemen got out and walked directly into the entranceway of the building where I had just been. Someone had called the police! Rev said he hadn't called them. Deanna hadn't called them. Who had? Who? Within moments they came back out and stopped to talk to some little kids playing on the sidewalk. There were no adults in sight. Who had called them? Someone must have seen or heard something!

Rev must have sensed my fear when I saw the police. Maybe he had heard the last threat.

"Whether you go to the clinic or not is up to you, Debbie," he said. "But you should know that if you go there, they'll automatically call the police.

Although I was still frightened for all of our lives, the threats somehow did not ring quite so strongly in my ears now that he was out of sight. But I couldn't talk. Not yet. Not to the police. Not to anyone. I was numb. I couldn't move. I ached. From deep inside a message pulsated through me. *You have to talk to the police.* But get out of the van? Back onto that street where that guy and his friends could see me talking to them? No. I would go to the clinic. The police would be called. I would talk to them. But later. *Please get me away from here. Take me anywhere. Just get me out of here. Take me away. Please.*

"Do you want me to take you to the clinic?" Rev asked.

It was all I could do to respond with one word . . . "Yes."

3

By the time they began their questioning, I felt nothing. What they perceived as calmness was actually a numbing quietude brought on by shock.

Deanna went with me into the clinic while Rev parked the van. But when I entered the waiting room, I began to wonder what I was doing there. I had never been a patient in a hospital before. Hospitals had always given me the creeps, especially emergency wards. . . . Why was I here? I had no broken bones. As far as the receptionist could tell, I was just fine.

"Yes, may I help you?"

"I need to see a doctor."

"What is this for?"

"I just . . . need to see a doctor."

"I'm sorry, but I have to know what this is for."

"I was raped."

The words fell to the pit of my stomach like dead weights. Hearing myself speak those three words was . . . that disgusting four-letter word was me. *Rape. Me. Oh, my God, I don't believe it.*

"Right this way, please."

I was taken to a very small examining room and handed a white paper gown. "Take all your clothes off please. The doctor will be in to see you shortly."

All my clothes? Everything? Oh, please, couldn't I just leave my underpants on?

It was so cold in there. Cotton balls in a jar. Tongue depressors in a taller glass jar. Gauze. *What am I doing here? I don't need any of this stuff. . . . Somebody get me out of here. Take me home. The lights are so bright.*

As I heard the doorknob turn, my heart pounded. A doctor and nurse entered.

"Lie down, please, and put your feet in the stirrups."

He walked around to the side of the table and lifted the paper gown. His cold hands pressed against my breast. A swelling scream from deep inside wanted to burst out of me. *Don't touch me! Can't you see I'm okay? You don't have to touch me!*

37

Get your hands off me! Oh, God, get me off this table! I'm trapped.
My feet are stuck. I can't move. Get away from me.

"Since you are still having your period," the doctor said,
"the chances of your getting pregnant are pretty slim."

Pregnant! I could be pregnant!

"In two weeks I want you to go to your regular doctor. He'll
need to do a test for venereal disease."

It hadn't occurred to me that *he* might have had venereal
disease.

"Have you ever had a pelvic exam before?"

"No."

"Well, just relax."

Relax! Relax? Oh, God. Rape. Pregnant. Venereal disease. Get
your fingers out of me. It's my body. Let me go. Don't you touch me!
Leave me alone! Oh, God, I can't bear this!

Although I felt like a living volcano with an eruption
brewing on the inside, to the doctors and nurses I must have
appeared extremely calm. I spoke quietly and only when
necessary to answer questions. My thoughts and emotions were
so jumbled that I began to lose touch with reality. I felt myself
giving in . . . as if a part of life had left me . . . that part of
me that wanted to fight back—to resist all that was happening
to me—left me. Powerless. I was not a part of what was going
on. It was all happening to me . . . without me.

Two policemen were brought into the examining room, the
same two we had seen at the apartment building. They must
have followed us to the clinic. As they asked their probing
questions, I answered them calmly. I sat on the examining
table naked, covered only by a paper as thin as the page on
which these words are printed. It never occurred to me that I
could have refused to talk to them. It never occurred to me
that I might have asked to get dressed before talking to them.
I had lost all control over my own welfare.

"Your name is Deborah Marston?"

"Yes."

"Is that spelled D-e-b-o-r-a-h M-a-r-s-t-o-n?"

"Yes."

"How old are you?"

"Nineteen."

"Your address?"

"Which one?"

"You have more than one?"

"I'm just living here in the city for the summer."

"Well, we better have both."

I told them what they wanted to know.

"What time did this happen?"

"I don't know."

"Can you give us an approximate time?"

"About forty-five minutes ago."

"About 7:30 then?"

"I guess so."

"Can you tell us what happened?"

"We were delivering—"

"Who's we?"

"Deanna and I."

He turned to his partner, "That's the black girl in the lobby
. . . go on."

"We were delivering some notices to tell the people that
church services would be moved to the Boys' Club tomorrow
. . . he followed me across the street into the apartment
building."

"Who's he? Do you know him?"

"No."

"You don't know his name, then?"

"No. Yes. He said it was Joe. Joe Namath or something like
that."

"Joe Namath?" They both laughed. "Do you know who Joe Namath is?"

"No."

"He's a football player for the New York Jets."

I was still in shock. I felt nothing. It wouldn't be until much later when I recalled their questions and their laughter that I would suffer further humiliation and embarrassment.

"Go on."

"I couldn't get out the door."

"What door?"

"The door to the apartment building."

"You were inside the building?"

"Yes. Just inside."

"And he was too?"

"Yes. He followed me in."

"Deanna was with you?"

"No, we had split up."

"What happened next?"

"He slammed me up against the wall. He put his hands up . . . my shirt."

"Go on."

"I told him I had VD. I tried to faint. He dragged me down the stairs."

"Go on."

"He raped me."

"Where were you—in the basement?"

"Yes, but just at the bottom of the stairs."

"Did you take your own clothes off?"

"No. He told me to, but I didn't."

"He took your clothes off then?"

"Just my pants."

"Did he have a gun?"

"No."

"Any weapon?"

"A knife."

"He pulled it on you?"

"No."

"You didn't see it?"

"No. But he kept reaching for it in his back pocket. He said he didn't want to hurt me."

"He threatened you?"

"Yes."

"What else did he say?"

"He said he knew where I lived. He said he'd get me if I didn't say I was his girl friend."

"Did he climax?"

"Uh, what do you mean?"

"Are you a . . . uh, were you a virgin?"

"Yes."

He turned to his partner, "She would have known if he had gone off."

"He didn't get any pleasure out of it, if that's what you mean. He wasn't finished with me. He was going to take me to his party."

"What party?"

"He said he was having a party. Some of his friends were across the street waiting for him."

"So did he take you across the street to his party?"

"No. Rev came."

"Oh, yeah, the minister. Did you climax . . . uh, have an orgasm?"

"No."

"Have you had intercourse with anyone else today?"

"No."

"Oh, yeah, you said you were a virgin. You understand we have to ask these questions. Uh, could you identify this guy?"

"I don't know."

"Was he black?"

"No."

"Chicano?"

"No, white."

"How tall?"

"Just a little taller than me."

"How tall are you?"

"Five-seven."

"Okay, say five-ten, then?"

"I guess so."

"Hair color?"

"Brown. And curly."

"How much did he weigh?"

"I don't know. He was sort of skinny."

"Any scars or marks on him?"

"I don't think so."

"Did you scratch him?"

"No."

"Did you kick or bite him?"

"No."

He turned again to his partner, "These do-gooders who come here think they're gonna change this place. They're just not tough enough. Some of them get raped three or four times before they finally leave."

Then he turned back to me, "What makes you so calm, anyway?"

"I had help." What I meant was that I had prayed throughout the rape and God had been helping me. But at that moment I didn't really care whether they understood what I meant. They didn't ask, and I didn't try to explain.

God truly had helped me through it, and I was thankful that Rev had not brought in a bloody, screaming, hysterical, half-dead victim, which was what the policemen expected to see. By the time they began their questioning, I felt nothing. What they perceived as calmness was actually a numbing quietude brought on by shock. Unfortunately, this would make my case all the more difficult to prove in court.

A lot of what took place immediately after the police questioning is buried forever. I don't remember getting dressed or leaving the hospital. I don't remember going back to our apartment, to Rev's house. I can only vaguely recall riding home from the city that same night to tell my parents what had happened. I do remember, though, a piece of conversation that Rev and I had on that trip home. . . .

"Do you think you'll come back?" he asked.

"I . . . don't know." Silence prevailed as I let my thoughts work their way through. "I want to . . . I think. I don't know what my parents will say."

"I called them to tell them I was bringing you home. I just told them you weren't feeling well."

"Oh. What if they don't want me to come back? What about Deanna? Do you think she would stay? By herself?"

"I don't know."

It was after midnight by the time we got to my home. I remember the look on both of my parents' faces when we walked in; they knew something was very wrong. It was Rev who actually told them.

"I wanted to bring her home so you could see that she's okay. Debbie was . . . raped tonight."

My mother's gasp drew my eyes from the floor to her face. I wished I hadn't looked at her at that moment. In my mind, I can still see her expression of shock and horror.

I don't remember any more of the conversation that took

place between my parents and Rev. I remember that my father saw Rev to the door and thanked him for bringing me home, but the rest is lost. I couldn't have remembered it the next day. The shock erased it all.

"We should write it all down, all the details," my father said after Rev left.

"What?" Exhaustion had set in. I just wanted to go to bed.

"Do you remember when I had that bad car accident? It took six years for that to get to court. Then I had to recall every detail—what I was wearing, exactly what moment I put my foot on the brakes, everything. Better to write it down while it's still fresh in your mind."

At that moment, it seemed like the most horrible thing my father had ever asked me to do. Cruel and heartless. But I was too numb to argue. My mother went to bed, and my father and I stayed up until five in the morning. He asked the questions and wrote down everything I said as I let him draw it all out of me.

Later, I was grateful that it had been written down. My father's notes were much more detailed than the police report. Later when I went to court, I didn't have to go through the anguish of trying to remember all that had happened. It was all down on paper. I would read it over and over to refresh my memory until the details became embedded in my mind.

But telling everything to my father was much more difficult than telling the police. I had never before shared the private aspects of my life with him. Describing the intimate details of what had happened left me feeling naked in front of him. I would have to tell my story many times, but that time was the most difficult.

4

Most of what Dave had to deal with at the time of my rape and soon thereafter was me, not the rape itself. He spent most of his energies in helping me through it.

Because I was still in shock, nothing that happened during the next few days is in my conscious memory. Somehow I got from Saturday, July fifth, the day of the rape, to the following Thursday, July tenth. It was to have been my day off, and Dave was coming to see me. Maybe that was why it was the first day I remembered.

My parents suggested that I stay upstairs for a few minutes after he arrived. They would explain to him that I had been a witness to a crime and was still a bit shaken so that I might not seem quite myself. They would also ask him not to question me about it.

It seemed somewhat awkward, but I did agree to it. And it did seem to relieve some of the pressure I felt. Even though Dave and I had only been dating each other for four months, I knew I must tell him that I had been raped—and soon. But I wasn't quite sure how he would react or when the time would be right. My parents' plan gave me temporary escape. I was free to enjoy the day with Dave, free to feel more like myself again . . . or so I thought.

We had planned to spend the day in downtown Chicago at a couple museums. As we were putting together our picnic lunch, Dave suggested that we save the Museum of Science and Industry for the afternoon and go to the aquarium first. We could have our lunch on the lawn at the aquarium, which is exactly what we did, surprisingly enough. I say that because our dates often were unplanned, and even the dates we planned would frequently get changed on the spur of the moment. But this time everything went according to schedule.

It was a beautiful day. The sun was warm, and Lake Michigan looked so inviting. The aquarium was located on a point extending out into the lake, so we could watch the kids playing on the beach as we sat on the lawn eating our tuna sandwiches and chips. It had been a pleasant morning.

Museums had never interested me much before, but now I was with Dave and away from the trauma of the rape, free to enjoy. Maybe somehow everything would be all right again.

As we walked hand in hand across the parking lot to the car, I was stunned. There, driving toward us, were my parents. At first anger hit me. What were they doing, checking up on us? Were they following us? How had they found us in this city of three million people? And then, almost as suddenly, fear struck. No, they weren't here to check up on us. They were here to get me. The police must have found the guy who had raped me.

Dave had spotted them, too. "What are *they* doing here?" he asked.

"I'm not sure. I'll see what they want."

I left Dave at his car and walked over to where my parents had stopped, a short distance away. As I leaned down to the window on the passenger side, my mother said, "We're sorry to interrupt your day. Looks like you've been having a good time."

"Yeah. What's up? How did you find us?"

"I heard you mention you might stop here for lunch. . . . The police picked him up. He's being held at the precinct station. We had to come and get you because they can only hold him for a few hours. They want you to identify him."

Oh, no. I don't want to see him again . . . please.

"How did they find him?" I asked.

"Well, the policeman who called us said Reverend Quillan saw him on the street and called them. They picked him up right away."

Reality forced itself on me. We were to follow my parents to the precinct station, but Dave still had no idea what was going on. I walked back to him, trying to figure out what to say.

"Dave, I'm sorry, but we have to skip the other museum."

"That's okay. What's wrong?"

"I have to go to a police station to identify someone. I don't know where it is, but we can follow my parents."

That was all I said, and Dave asked no questions. It was all I could do to keep up a superficial conversation on the way to the station. My thoughts were tearing me apart. I would have to see *him* again, face to face. *Maybe it's not him. Maybe they got the wrong guy. What if I'm not* sure *it's him?*

My father and I went into the big stone building, leaving Dave and my mother sitting out in my dad's car. We were taken to a back room and were told that I would be looking through a screen through which I could see the suspect, but he would not be able to see me. As I waited for him to be brought into the room, the tension built inside me. When I saw him enter the room, my body became hot all over and I could actually feel the color drain from my face. I had lost all movement, all life. Somehow, I managed to nod my head to the policeman. I could not utter a sound. It was him. There was no doubt.

Although his eyes never met mine, even through the impenetrable mesh I was stricken with fear that he could see me. All his threats came back to me now. He was only a few feet away. He could reach out and touch me. Only the screen separated us. It didn't matter that I was standing in a police station with all kinds of protection around me. There had been people on the street only a few yards away from where he had raped me. No one had prevented that. Suddenly it was as if only he and I were there. My terror incapacitated me. Only after he was taken out of my sight did I gain control.

I don't remember how I got from there to the next room. I didn't pass out, but I was in such a state of shock that much of my own physical movement took place without any conscious knowledge on my part. When I returned to reality, I was seated in a larger room that had many backless benches in it—some sort of briefing or meeting room for the policemen.

"Would you like a glass of water?" I looked up. Standing in front of me, holding out a glass of cold water, was an officer I had not seen before.

"Thank you." I was extremely grateful for his thoughtfulness. It was only a small kindness, but it was as if someone had lit a candle for me in a huge, vast, dark room. The blackness had been pierced. I was beginning to see again. I was regaining control. I could function now.

In order for the police to hold the assailant, I had to sign a formal complaint, which meant going over all the details again. I also had to decide whether I would prosecute. This decision was all the more difficult to make because of the horror of seeing him again. The idea of coming face to face with him in court was unbearable. And what of all those threats? If I prosecuted, he would find out all about me and how to get me.

Maybe it was the policeman's assurances that this guy was as scared as I was, maybe the fear that people wouldn't believe me if I backed out now, or maybe the scratching for survival from way inside that spoke to me saying, "Press on. Do something. If you stop now, you'll die. You have to fight to stay alive." Somehow God provided me with sufficient strength to make the decision to go ahead with it.

The whole procedure took over two hours, and as my father and I left the building, it suddenly hit me that Dave and my mother were still out in my parents' car. When I saw Dave, I wondered if she had told him. "Let's talk when we get home," I said to him as we walked back to his car. Bumper-to-bumper rush-hour traffic, the afternoon heat, and the exhaustion that was setting in made the trip home long and unpleasant. I couldn't believe that my morning and afternoon fit into the same day. For the first time, I was forced to place my growing love for Dave, and the joy that brought, side by side with the ugliness of the rape. I could no longer separate them into two worlds. Both were a part of my life, and somehow I had to learn to put them together.

My parents had arrived home shortly before Dave and I did, and Dave waited in the car while I went into the house. I found my mother in the kitchen.

"Dave and I are going over to the church to talk."

"You're going to tell him?" she asked.

"I have to. I have to explain what happened this afternoon, and I'm not going to lie to him. Don't hold supper for us."

"I doubt the church is open—"

I was already out the door.

Our church was only six blocks away. It was too short a ride to cram in all the praying I wanted to do on the way. *Oh, Lord, please give me the words to tell him. If he falls apart, please give me the strength to handle that. If he's angry, please help me to calm him. If he turns cold and no longer wants me, please help me to bear that. Oh, Lord, what will he say? How will he react? Please help me, Father. . . .*

When we arrived at the church, the doors were locked. As we turned to try another entrance, I continued praying. *Dear Lord, now I'm asking You for a place to tell Dave. Please let it be my church. Please find a way.* As we were walking away, the door behind us opened. The custodian was leaving for the day . . . and it had to be the grumpy one. Somehow we were able to convince this very reluctant keeper of the house that we were trustworthy church members (even though Dave was not a member there) in need of a place to talk, and he let us in. I considered that a very definite, positive answer to my prayer, as I had had problems in the past trying to use the church when there were not "adults" around.

As we entered the sanctuary, I was immediately comforted by its quiet beauty. The afternoon sun pouring through the stained-glass window at the front of the sanctuary radiated its colors throughout the huge room. The chancel was raised up a level of three steps, and it was on these steps that Dave and I seated ourselves. When I look back on it now, it seems so right that we should have been there, so near to the cross, the symbol of both suffering and redemption.

"What did my parents tell you this morning . . . about what happened in the projects?" I began, my heart pounding.

"They just said that you had witnessed some sort of crime or something."

"Well, that's not exactly true. Did my mother tell you anything else when you were waiting in the car with her?"

"No. We listened to the Cub game and talked about other stuff." I could tell by the look on his face that he sensed the seriousness of the situation.

"This isn't my day off today, Dave. I've been home since Saturday night, and I don't think I'm going back."

"You're quitting your job?"

"I'm . . . not sure. I think so."

"Why?"

"I was more than just a witness to a crime . . . I was raped."

"Oh . . . Debbie. . . ." He put his arms around me and held me for a long time . . . in silence. I could feel his tears soak into the shoulder of my blouse. Finally he spoke. "But I don't understand. I prayed so hard for you."

"I know."

We held each other as if letting go would bring the world crashing in. Then, Dave broke the embrace. He lifted my chin so that our eyes met—and spoke once more.

"Debbie, there's something I want you to know. . . . Nothing in the world can ever change my love for you."

5

Roger Gray, you stole something from me, but I don't know what to call it. You left me with a feeling, a feeling I can't explain. It's as if when you raped me, you threw me into a deep, dark pit.

My first court appearance was scheduled for Friday, July 11, the day after I had identified the rapist. I had done my homework, going over and over the details of the rape in my mind. *I have to get every last detail right or they won't believe me. If my story has changed even in the slightest, they'll think I'm lying. They'll believe him—him! And not me. I've prepared my mind. But oh, my God, I'm not ready.* How could this have happened to me? I couldn't believe it was me. It must be happening to someone else. It was like a bad TV show. If only I could just turn it off. Just turn it off and walk away.

I decided to wear a plain brown dress. It would show respect for the court to wear a dress, and this one was simple and modest. They couldn't think I asked for it or wanted it. They couldn't think that of me, could they? *They don't know me. They don't even know me!*

I stood beside the car staring up at the massive building across the street. *He* was somewhere inside that building. I quickly looked away. My mother stood waiting for my father as he dug in his pocket for parking meter money. What a trivial thing to have to worry about! We were trying to avoid a parking ticket while in a few minutes I had to stand in front of a judge and tell him I was raped. And *he* would be right there! *Oh, my God, why does he have to be there?*

What if I fall apart when I see him? What if I freeze? What if I can't even talk? What if he threatens me again? He could have a knife hidden in his sock! They always search prisoners, don't they? Don't they?

The lobby of the building was crowded with people. Prosecutors, defense attorneys, victims, criminals. But who was who? I couldn't tell. What did I look like to them? In just a few minutes an entire courtroom of strangers would know . . . they would know that I had been raped.

The courtroom was on the fourth floor. My parents and I

barely fit into an already packed elevator. The doors closed. I couldn't move. What if he was in there too? What if the guy who raped me was in the same elevator? *I can't get out. I'm trapped! I can't even move. I have to look at everyone in this elevator. I can't see everyone. They're all staring at me. But I have to turn around to see. I have to see if he's in this elevator!*

I was the first one out when the heavy doors split their seams. I stood and watched as the crowd of people emptied through the opening. No, he had not been on the elevator. Thank God. But when would I have to see him? What if I just bumped into him in the hall?

". . . the big double doors on the left at the end of the hall."

"Thank you."

This hall was buzzing with movement, too. People going every direction. Some carrying briefcases, some wiping noses of noisy, impatient children, some, like us, simply walking . . . not knowing what lay ahead for them that day.

The courtroom was hot and noisy. It wasn't at all like Perry Mason or the Defenders. A lady was changing a baby's diaper on one of the back benches. A baby? In a place like this? Coming toward me was a tall bleach-blonde wearing a black leather miniskirt and vest and white vinyl go-go boots. The room reeked of stale cigars. Flies buzzed in through the open windows. Instead of dress shirts, most of the men in the room were wearing dirty white T-shirts. One of them even had a pack of cigarettes rolled up in his sleeve!

We found a place about five rows from the front. My parents sat on either side of me, my father nearest the center aisle. Almost as soon as we were seated, a uniformed policeman sat down next to my father.

"Are you Mr. Marston?"

"Yes."

56

"I'm Officer Farrell."

My father had talked to him on the phone; he had called to tell us to be here today. He was also the arresting officer in my case.

"They have a few more cases before ours. Shouldn't be long, though."

A young kid dressed in blue jeans, a T-shirt, and a leather vest was brought in and placed directly in front of the judge.

"State your name." He did. "Your age."

"Fourteen."

"It says here that you assaulted Officer Thompson with a knife. Is that true?"

"Yes, sir."

"Have you ever been in trouble before?"

"No, sir."

With people all around us talking and rustling in their seats, it was difficult to hear the whole conversation. But I strained to hear as much as I could.

"I don't ever want to see you in my courtroom again. Do you understand?"

"Yes, sir."

"All right. Get out of here."

That was it. He was released. I watched the officer who had been assaulted as his face flushed with anger and frustration. Shaking his head in disgust, he turned and walked away.

I couldn't believe it! This kid had attacked a policeman with a knife, and he got a quick slap on the hand and was put back on the street. Is that what they would do to the guy who raped me? A slap on the hand and back on the street?

Two more cases were heard and then . . .

"The State of Illinois vs. Roger Gray."

Officer Farrell stood up, looked at me, and said, "That's us."

So that was his name. Roger Gray. No one had told me what his name really was. As I moved out into the aisle, the side door opened and an officer led Roger Gray to the front. I placed myself as far from him as I could, with my father and two other men between us. As they spoke, I figured out that one was the defense attorney and the other was the district attorney who would be representing me. The district attorney spoke first.

"Your honor, we have not yet received the medical report from the crime lab, which is essential to our case. We wish to implore a continuance."

Turning to the defense attorney, the judge inquired, "Objection?"

"No, your honor."

"Two weeks. Hearing is set for 9:00 A.M., July 25."

The judge then addressed Roger Gray. "Since you don't have a record, bail is reduced to $5,000. Next case."

That was it? It was over? I was confused. What happened? As we turned to leave, Officer Farrell suggested to my father that we go to the coffee shop across the street from the courthouse to talk.

It was smoke-filled and packed with people. By the time we found a table, I was bursting with questions.

"Was that man in the three-piece suit my lawyer?"

"Yes, that was the district attorney. He'll be presenting your case."

"Shouldn't I talk to him? He doesn't even know me."

"He couldn't possibly take time to talk to all the plaintiffs. He goes through a case every half-hour in there. Besides, he has your statement and all the reports."

"So why didn't he say anything else? I thought I'd have to tell the whole story today."

"No, Debbie. Do you remember those tests they took at the hospital?"

"What tests?"

"Well, they took one that should show the presence of sperm."

"Oh." Suddenly I became anxious, fidgeting with a napkin. Anyone could overhear our conversation.

"Those results haven't come back yet, so the district attorney asked for a continuance. That just means the hearing is delayed for two weeks or more."

"What do you mean, 'or more'?" my voice softened.

"Well, Roger Gray's attorney can ask for a continuance, too, if he wants to."

"Why would *he* want to?"

"Oh, just to have more time to prepare his defense. Sometimes it's a delay tactic. They figure if they can put it off, maybe you'll decide to drop the charges."

"How did he get that lawyer?" I asked.

"Beats me. His folks aren't even in town. They're on vacation. But he wasn't appointed by the court. That's his own lawyer."

"I didn't figure anyone in the projects could afford one. I don't understand why he gets to have his own lawyer and I don't."

"Well, see, rape is a crime against the state, so the state represents you. The district attorney will do fine. Don't worry."

"Well, at least he'll be in jail. (Later I learned that Roger Gray did raise the bail money and had spent only one night in jail.) Why did the judge reduce the bail? When I identified him, they told me he had a record."

"No. See, he's been arrested three times before. Once for grand theft, once for possession of narcotics, and I don't know what else. But they've never gotten a conviction on him. So the judge reduced it to $5,000. It had been set at $10,000. . . . Say, Debbie, there is something you should think about. They'll probably try to get you to change your mind about the charge."

"About the charge? What do you mean?"

"Well, if you change it to assault rather than rape, they might have a better chance of convicting him."

"What do you mean? He didn't beat me up . . . he raped me! Why should I change it to assault?"

"Just think about it, Debbie."

Officer Farrell had been right about two things. The district attorney did try to get me to reduce the charge to assault. I refused. And on July 25, Roger Gray's attorney did ask for a continuance. It was granted.

My third court appearance was on August 14, the preliminary hearing. The defense attorney asked for another continuance. He was definitely stalling. He must have known Deanna would not be available to testify in a couple of weeks.

"Your honor," the district attorney spoke in my defense, "Deanna Harris, one of our key witnesses, is spending her junior year in college abroad. She leaves for France on September 9. The defense has had five weeks to prepare its case."

"We shall proceed with the hearing. Request for continuance denied."

I was directed to stand right next to Roger Gray, facing the judge. Mentally I put up a wall between us. Just because I had to stand next to him did not mean I had to look at him or even recognize that he was there. I would not.

The judge directed the first question to me.

"State your name, please."

My heart pounded. Part of my wall was coming down. Now he was going to find out who I was.

"Debbie Marston," I mumbled.

"Speak up please, young lady."

"Deborah Marston."

"How old are you?"

"Nineteen."

"It says you're a college student. What college do you attend?"

More of my wall crumbled . . . he'd know how to find me!

Before I could make myself say the words, my father, who had been standing behind me, interrupted. "Your honor, Debbie would rather not answer that question with *him* right here."

"You're the girl's father?"

"Yes."

The judge turned back to me. "You will answer the question, Deborah."

I spoke softly. "Godwin College."

The judge's response came loud and clear. "Godwin College. Never heard of it. Where is it?"

What do you want from me? Why are you asking me *all the questions? Why don't you ask this Roger Gray something? He raped* me! *I didn't rape* him!

Bit by bit, question after question, my wall collapsed. I was stripped down . . . no protection, no defenses, naked in front of him once more. *Oh, God, he's doing it again. He's getting me again. Get me out of here. Oh, God, get me out. . . .*

Officer Farrell told me afterwards that the purpose of the hearing had been for the judge to decide whether or not there was sufficient evidence to proceed with the case. But I never understood why so much personal information had to be revealed. Maybe the judge had been testing me to see if I was serious about it and willing to go through with a trial. Whatever his reasons, he decided to send it on to the grand jury. The date was set for one week later.

Dear Lord, You got me through the rape. Please help me now.

By the time my parents and I walked up the endless steps inside the courthouse to the lobby, I was winded. Deanna and Rev were already there. They would be testifying in front of the grand jury today as well. As we walked toward them, I noticed a woman that I had not seen before with them. Deanna turned to introduce her to us.

"Debbie, Mr. and Mrs. Marston, this is my mother."

It wasn't until that moment that it occurred to me that this had been a rough experience for Deanna and Rev too. I had been so wrapped up in getting myself through all of it that I had not considered the effect it would have on them. I began to appreciate what it had taken for them to even be there to support me in prosecuting Roger Gray. Deanna's mother lived 250 miles away, yet had come to be with her daughter for the grand jury hearing.

A voice interrupted my thoughts. "Come this way please." We were led down a dimly lit hallway, closed off from the rest of the building, and were asked to wait on a wooden bench in the hall just outside the courtroom. Deanna was called in first.

My stomach was churning. I was wearing the same brown dress I had worn to court before. Fidgeting with one of the buttons, I began to let some of my nervousness out.

"I don't know if I can do this. What's taking them so long in there, anyway?" *What am I doing here? Do I have to tell them everything? What if I can't answer their questions? I didn't know what climax was before. What if they ask me stuff like that again? Dear Lord, you got me through the rape. Please help me now.*

At that moment of confusion, frustration, nervousness, and fear, strength sufficient for the hour came through my mother's words.

"Debbie, just do it for the other twenty-five girls he might rape if they don't get him off the street."

The thought grabbed my scattering fears. I might be saving

somebody else from a rape by going through this now. It gave me a purpose, a reason to go on. I would cling to that thought throughout the questioning.

The massive courtroom door opened and Deanna came out. I was motioned to go in. As we passed each other, I whispered to her, "How'd it go?"

She managed a weak smile, "Okay, I guess."

As I entered the courtroom full of people, I saw only two familiar faces, the district attorney and the defense attorney. After being sworn in, I was directed to sit on a straight-backed chair in a boxed-in area, this time similar to the Perry Mason courtroom. The judge was sitting to my right, above and slightly behind me.

Directly in front of me was the jury. Fifteen men and women. They were seated behind three rows of raised senate-like desks, covering the whole width of the room. All eyes were focused on me.

The judge instructed me to relate my story. It had been well-rehearsed. Maybe too well-rehearsed. I told everything in detail, including conversation between Roger Gray and myself. The questions followed.

"Please clarify when it was that he kissed you on the street," a jury member asked.

"It was right after he raped—"

"Objection, your honor," the defense attorney cut in.

The judge spoke to the jury. "The jury will recognize 'alleged' rape."

"Will you please describe what was happening between the time Miss Harris left and the time she returned with Reverend Quillan?" the same jury member asked.

"He was . . . raping me."

"Objection!" Roger Gray's attorney had jumped to his feet and yelled his objection, startling me.

This time the judge turned to me, "Young lady, you will refrain from using the word 'rape.' Rape has not been proven. You will answer the question please."

"He was . . . in me."

"Did you see him enter you?"

"I was staring at the ceiling. I didn't watch."

"I see. Then it could have been with his finger or anything else that he entered you?"

There was a pause. The judge spoke to me, "You will answer the question."

"No, it wasn't anything else . . . it was him."

"But you didn't see?"

"No." *Would that mean I wasn't raped?*

"How old are you?" another jury member asked.

"Nineteen."

"It says here that he's seventeen."

Two years younger than me. He was younger than me! I didn't have the chance to say in defense that he looked much older. Kids in the city had mistaken me for fourteen. The hardness of the city had not had time to touch my face the way it had the young people who had grown up there . . . the way it had toughened him. All they heard was that I was nineteen and he was seventeen, two years my junior.

"How tall are you?"

"Five-feet-seven." I knew what they were thinking. He was only slightly taller.

"How much do you weigh?"

"125."

"It says here that he weighs less than that."

Why were they asking all this? They had all this information in front of them. What were they trying to prove? That I should have been able to overpower him? What about his buddies out in the street who were waiting for us? What about all the threats? All they wanted to know was who was bigger? What about the knife in his back pocket?

"Did you see his knife? Did he pull it on you?"

"No, but he kept reaching for it saying, 'I don't want to hurt you.' Over and over he said that."

"Did you see it?"

I couldn't believe it. Everyone knew that absolutely all the teen-age guys and girls in the projects carried knives, often switchblades. I had no reason to doubt that he had one in his pocket. Should it have occurred to me in that moment of terror for my life that this attacker might be younger, might weigh less, and might possibly be bluffing about a knife in his pocket?

"Did you actually see the weapon?"

"No!"

But it was there. . . . They didn't know! How could they know?

"Why didn't you ring the doorbells on the mailboxes?"

"I, uh, don't . . . know . . . I . . . guess I didn't think of it."

"Why didn't you scream?"

"I don't know."

The district attorney was given the floor. He asked only one question.

"Deborah, did you know Roger Gray before the day in question?"

"No, I had never seen him before."

The defense attorney asked only one question as well.

"Is it possible that Roger Gray could have known you?"

"I don't think—"

"Is it possible?"

"Well, I suppose he might have seen me—"

"That's all, your honor."

The judge turned to me. "Thank you. You may step down."

I was confused. Something wasn't right. When I was back in the hallway, a thought surfaced.

"Rev," I asked, "are there doorbells on the mailboxes in those apartment buildings?"

"No, why?"

"They tricked me! Oh, no! They asked why I didn't ring the doorbells on the mailboxes! Rev, you've gotta tell them there aren't any. When you go in there, could you tell them that? Please?"

"I'll do what I can, Debbie."

Rev was called in next. As I sat there on the bench waiting for him to come out, my anger grew like a cancer. After ten or fifteen minutes, he walked out looking pale.

"Did you tell them, Rev—about the doorbells?"

"No, Debbie, I didn't get a chance."

The district attorney soon joined us.

"Well, all we do is wait now," he said.

"What about Roger Gray? Doesn't he have to be here?" I asked.

"They heard his side of the case yesterday. They should have a decision before too long."

"You mean today? Right now?"

"Most likely. I'll be back as soon as I know something. It would probably be best if you all wait right here." With that, he went back down the long hall, the same way he had come.

Not more than fifteen or twenty minutes later, he returned.

"Mr. and Mrs. Marston and Deborah, will you come with me please?" Rev and Deanna and her mother were left on the bench in the hall, while he led us to a small conference room. Once there, he looked directly at me as he spoke.

"The jury reached their decision. They didn't indict him."

"There won't be a trial?"

"No."

"It's over?"

"Yes."

He won't go to jail, I thought to myself. Relief. Tremendous relief. The minimum sentence would have been twenty years, they had told me. Now I didn't have to worry that he might blame me for sending him to prison and come after me when he got out. . . . But—wait a minute. They believed him? Not me!

"They didn't believe me!"

"It's not a question of whether they believed you or not. They might very well have believed your story."

"What do you mean? You said they didn't indict him."

"Actually, they're doing you a favor by not going to trial with this case. They're saving you the trouble of going through all that. Their decision just means that they don't think there is sufficient evidence for a conviction."

"What do you mean? I had two witnesses!"

"Neither one saw the act itself. It was your word against—"

"But the hospital lab report proved penetration."

"Yes, but they couldn't prove it wasn't willing on your part. It's tough to convict on these cases. They don't usually get 'em unless they can hang up torn and bloody clothes for evidence. Usually then it goes to homicide anyway."

"They couldn't prove it wasn't willing on your part. . . . They couldn't prove it wasn't willing on your part. . . . They couldn't prove it wasn't willing. . . ." The words echoed through my head. What did I have to do? Show them scars and broken bones? All I wanted was to stay alive. Willing on my part? *Oh, my God. What do they think I am? What do they think I am?*

* * *

70

One of the questions asked by the grand jury that day remained unanswered for a long time, even in my own mind: Why didn't I scream? The answer was more complicated than any of the jury members could have imagined, and in order to answer it, I had to go back in my mind to that late afternoon in the projects. . . .

Deanna and I were more afraid of street brawls and gang fights than anything else. We knew that being out on those streets on a Saturday night after dark was quite dangerous. Besides, I had been brought up not to be out in any unsure situation after dark. It was that "after dark on the city streets" phenomenon that made Deanna and me decide to split up. We had a lot of leaflets to deliver. If we stayed together, we would not get home before the streets were unsafe. So we split up.

Even though it was the first time I had been alone on the inner-city streets, I felt relatively sure of myself. I was in my own neighborhood—not more than two blocks from Rev's house and our apartment. Deanna was on one side of the street and I was on the other. We could even see each other from time to time as we went from building to building. And the street was crawling with kids. Somehow there was a feeling of safety where children were playing.

With all the people on the street and Deanna close by, it didn't occur to me that I could be in danger . . . that I could be snatched at any moment and raped or killed in an entranceway to an apartment building. Besides, I was doing God's work. Nothing could happen to me. Not me. Not there. Not then. Not ever. God would take care of me.

I think it was this disbelief, this failure to recognize that anything so terrible could happen to me, that kept me, in part, from screaming. In the first few moments when I was confronted by Roger Gray, I did not allow myself to believe I was in danger. The moment he grabbed my breasts, I knew I was in real trouble, but by that time I was past the point of a reactionary scream—by that I mean the kind of scream you let loose when someone jumps out at you from behind a bush.

When reality did hit, it hit hard. My assailant had a knife. I was in his world, not mine. He had been drinking. *His* friends were waiting for him out on the street. *His* friends would come if I screamed. Or would anyone come? This was not my world. In my world if anything looked suspicious, someone would call the police, who would be there within a few minutes. This was not suburbia. This was the inner city of Chicago. Here they shouted, "Pigs!" at policemen driving by in their cruisers. Who would get involved? And even if someone did, how long would it take the police to come on a Saturday night? Sometimes it took a half-hour or more for them to answer a call. I could hear voices outside, but it did not mean help for me. Who would get involved—to help me?

Besides, if I screamed he might kill me. I couldn't get past him to get out the door. I couldn't talk him out of it. He didn't care if I had VD or my period. Fainting had not helped. He just dragged me down the stairs. If I screamed, he would shut me up. . . . *Please don't hurt me any more. I won't scream. Please don't kill me. I won't scream. Please. . . .*

Subconsciously, I was aware of all these elements at the time I was raped; yet when the jury member asked why I didn't scream, I had no answer. I had not been able to work through all of this. I just didn't know.

But none of this would matter. Finding the answers after the hearing couldn't change the outcome. It was over. A trial could have meant trips home from college for court appearances; it might have dragged on for a year or more. So I was set free as well. I would never have to see *him* again! *Oh, God, it's over. It's really all over!*

7

Everyone close to me had been damaged as well. Each had his or her
own feelings and emotions to deal
with, not unlike my own.

My days at home following the court proceedings passed quickly. Since the department store where I had worked the previous summer was in need of part-time help, I was able to get a job clerking four days a week. Much of my free time was spent in seeing friends from high school days, visiting Dave, and preparing for the return to college in the fall.

Though I managed to keep myself busy, this period of time at home did not pass without incident. We had all tried to leave the rape behind, never talking about it except when necessary.

Since my sister was only thirteen, my parents chose not to tell her what had happened to me. She didn't know about it until several years later when I told her myself. My older brother, Matt, knew soon after it happened. He and I were always close, and I wished I could spend more time with him. But his summer job at the railroad kept him away from home much of the time.

Both my parents and I wanted to shove the whole experience in the closet and close the door on it. Unfortunately, we could not. I didn't realize it at the time, but throughout the hearings I had been denying many of my own feelings about the rape itself in order to emotionally endure the ordeal. I had convinced myself that I was strong and in control when actually I had not faced the multitude of negative feelings that were yet to surface.

A perfect example of this denial is revealed in a portion of a letter I wrote to Dave just after the grand jury's decision.

> There's nothing to worry about any more. It's all over. Dave, I have never felt so grateful to be alive. I could have been killed. But God didn't let that happen. It feels so good just to be alive. Everything's going to be O.K. now.

My parents had denied many of their emotions as well, but this could not last. The night that my father's repressed anger over the rape was initially unleashed was a terrible night for all of us.

It was a Saturday night. I had gone to the basement to iron a blouse I needed for church the next day. It was early evening, and the heat of the day had not yet lifted its hold upon us. I stood over the ironing board, beads of sweat rolling down my temple past my ear. There was tension in the air—the kind that comes when humidity and heat drain from us such virtues as patience and even tolerance for one another. I felt as one does between the time the lightning flashes and the thunder claps in a violent storm. An uneasiness . . . a restlessness.

When the hard, fast footsteps stormed down the stairs, I knew I was the target of their approach. It was my father's feet that first spoke of his irrepressible anger as they deliberately shook each step of the stairs on the way down. A shudder crept down my spine.

My father's yelling was something I had learned to tolerate but could never get used to. As his rage tore through me, my body responded . . . my stomach beginning to churn, my arms and face becoming hot, my legs begging to be relieved of my body's weight. But I would take this standing up.

"What were you doing out there at night? You should have known better! If you hadn't been out there, it never would have happened!"

"I was doing my job! It was my job to be there!"

I couldn't believe it. He was blaming me. It was not my fault! I never asked Roger Gray to rape me! . . . *I am not a slut. You can't blame me. I won't let you!*

Never in my life had I ever yelled back at my father. Even now I couldn't scream at him, except in my mind. But I could do the next best thing . . . and I did. I walked out on him in the midst of his explosion of anger. I yanked the cord of the iron from the socket. Without a single word, I glared hate at him, then briskly and feverishly escaped by way of the basement door.

I would never go back there. He was not my father. He was hateful . . . mean . . . cruel. I would never see him or speak to him again. As the door slammed behind me, I could still hear yelling.

"Where do you think you're going?"

"Well, she needs somebody," my brother accused.

"Don't you press her for any details."

I was half a block away when Matt caught up with me. We walked together in silence. All my energy was being consumed by my muscles, held tight in tension. Gradually my speech took over the job of letting the anger out.

"I'm never going back there, ever."

"He's just angry, Debbie. He'll cool off."

"Just angry? He blamed me for it. He thinks it's all *my* fault!"

"Give him some time, Debbie. He doesn't know how to deal with all this."

"Why should *I* have to be the one to give to *him?* What about me? Doesn't he care at all about me?"

"I think he feels really guilty, Debbie."

"Guilty? For what?"

"For letting you go there."

"That's stupid. That was my decision. It was my job. I should be back there right now. I don't know how Deanna's doing it all herself."

"He could have insisted that you couldn't go in the first place. He must wish he had now. Debbie, I just think he couldn't face blaming himself, so he blew up at you."

"Great. That's just great. So why doesn't mother say anything? She never talks about it."

"I don't know, Debbie. I just don't know."

We walked for what seemed like three or four miles. It was past the time when you could hear mothers calling from their front doors, "Didn't you see the streetlight go on? Time to come in."

Somehow as Matt and I talked, I was able to calm down enough so that my anger turned to hurt and terrible disappointment. Not only did I have to face the fact of being raped, but now my own father was blaming me for it—blaming me for all the shame, the humiliation, the pain, the terror, all the awful things I was feeling. They were not caused by something I had done. They were caused by what Roger Gray had done to me. Yet my father was blaming me and my mother couldn't talk about it. I couldn't handle it all. It would be easier to simply reject my parents.

But I couldn't face a separation from them at this point in my life, either. If I walked out on my family now, I would have no one else to turn to . . . nowhere to go. I was too terrified to go back to the city. Besides, I was still a part of my father's household. I couldn't bear to lose my home on top of everything else.

When we got back to the house, I took a deep breath and slowly climbed the seven cement steps leading to the front door. The squeak of the screen door announced my arrival. My father did not look up as I walked over to the chair where he was sitting. It had been a long time since I had kissed my father. Physical affection was not often shown between us. It took every muscle in my body to lean over and place my kiss on his cheek. He sat firmly planted in his chair and did not speak. Nor did I.

I went directly to my room. There I began to sort out all the feelings that had surfaced. When I kissed my father, I had felt a kind of power rise within me. In spite of all that he had done to me, I was able to come back . . . to forgive him with a kiss.

My kiss must have humiliated him, made him feel sorry for what he had said. Was that forgiveness? Or was it retaliation? Deep inside, I think I wanted it to be both.

I had not been the only victim of Roger Gray's rape. Everyone close to me had been damaged as well. Each had his or her own feelings and emotions to deal with, not unlike my own. Unfortunately, at that time I desperately needed their support.

Being a parent myself now, I can look back with a certain appreciation for what my parents must have been going through. They had their own shock, disgust, and guilt to handle as well as having to deal with me. But at the time I was bitterly angry and emotionally devastated by my father's outburst. It hurt for a long time. I could more easily reject him than accept his limitations. He was not a person who could cry his feelings out in tears. Nor was it easy for him to talk about them. When his feelings were finally released in anger, I was their target since I was the one who had brought the crisis home.

Not until several years later was I able to fully forgive my father for blaming me for the rape. Before I could take that step, I had to acknowledge that he would not always live up to my expectations of him.

It wasn't the first time I had come to this realization about my father. At the tender age of seven I had been forced to see that he was not a god . . . that he was human. I think that realization hurt more than anything else—more than skinned knees, more than my brother's socks in the arm. Until that time, my father had been infallible. The realization came through an experience my brother Matt and I shared one summer. . . .

One day Matt and I were at a loss for things to do. We managed to get into a "my dad's bigger than your dad" conversation with Jimmy, one of the neighbor kids. He and my brother were in the second grade together. When Jimmy bragged that his dad ate chocolate-covered ants and frog legs, Matt was not to be outdone. Spotting a yellowjacket buzzing by, he replied, "Well, my dad eats bee sandwiches."

"He does not."

"He does so."

"Does not."

"Does so. Go ask him."

I was so intent on proving my brother right and my father the hero Matt was making him out to be that I actually allowed myself to believe it was true. Our small, but brand-new house had a huge, treeless back yard, and the grass was filled with clover which attracted all kinds of bees. Maybe my father did eat bee sandwiches. I chimed into the bickering, sticking up for my brother all the way into the house.

We found my dad, who promptly said that sure, he loved bee sandwiches, but that he wouldn't eat one unless it had *fifty* bees in it. I imagine he thought that would put an end to the bickering. Obviously, my father had not spent as much time in the back yard as we had. We knew we could find fifty bees if we really tried. On our way out, we stopped at the kitchen junk drawer and picked out three of the biggest, fattest rubber bands you ever saw.

"What are we going to do with these?" I asked, like a tag-along little sister.

"We're going bee hunting, stupid," Matt said.

Well, I wasn't too keen on that idea because I had been stung by a bee the summer before. It had made my whole face swell up, and I had been so sick from it that I had to stay in for a whole day. But my loyalty to my brother and my pride in my father won out over my fears. I took one of the makeshift slingshots and marched out right alongside my big brother on the big bee hunt.

By suppertime, we had collected forty-three bees, but my dad insisted that it wasn't a bee sandwich until we had fifty. We had a difficult time finding the last seven bees, but later that same evening we managed to present my dad with fifty yellowjackets and wasps. After they had been stunned by the slap of the rubber band, Matt had picked them up with a straight pin and stuck them to the bottom of an overturned cardboard box. When we handed the box to my dad, some of them were still squirming under their pins.

My father insisted that though he loved bees, he just didn't have the heart to eat any that were still moving. He suggested that we put them in the freezer and he would eat them the next day. I don't know how we could have agreed to that. The suspense was killing us. But we said we would wait until the next day.

Jimmy was knocking at our door early the next morning. The three of us stood around my dad with our big, round eyes bugging out of their sockets. First he spread butter on two slices of bread, then carefully placed each of the fifty bees on the buttered bread. As he put the top slice on the sandwich, he said, "You know, I'm really not hungry enough to eat it now. I'll eat it later." Three small sighs came out of three small bodies like air rushing out of a balloon.

"I'll just put it back in the freezer like this and have it later."

Sometime later that afternoon on one of our many trips back to the freezer to check on the sandwich, we found that it was gone. We ran to find my dad who said, "Yes, bee sandwiches sure are delicious."

Proud in his victory, Matt turned to Jimmy and uttered the

inevitable, "See, I told you so." It was like Peter Pan. We all believed. . . .

Two days later was garbage pickup day. The garbage cans had been taken out to the street as usual. It was there that Matt and I would sometimes scrounge through the trash to see if any of our junky but prized possessions had been thrown out. We were carefully thumbing through it when—we both gasped simultaneously in shock and disappointment. There, halfway down the can, partially stuck to the side, was the bee sandwich. He had not eaten it after all.

Needless to say, we never told Jimmy.

Recalling this incident several years later, I remembered those first feelings of disillusionment. By then I was old enough to understand that my father was human and that although he might sometimes hurt or disappoint me, he was still my father and he still loved me.

"Lord, please help me to stop expecting my father to be more than he is."

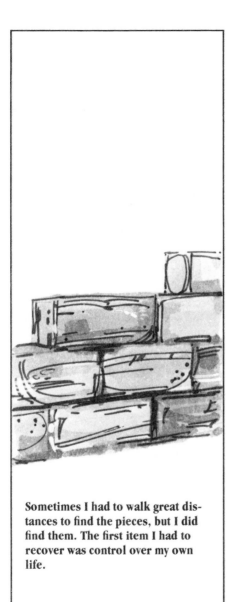

Sometimes I had to walk great distances to find the pieces, but I did find them. The first item I had to recover was control over my own life.

It was dark. Someone was chasing me. No. He wasn't running. Neither was I, but I was so out of breath! He was following me. I couldn't tell who it was . . . just a dark figure, a flowing, nondescript form. I tried to scream, but I couldn't make a sound. "I'm going to get you!" Closer . . . closer. . . . Suddenly I saw his face. At that same instant I saw the pistol. He grabbed me by the neck and I stopped breathing. The gun was pressed into my temple so hard that it hurt. It went off three times. I heard it blast right through my head.

I sat straight up in bed screaming. I had always thought that when you had nightmares you were supposed to wake up before you died. I guess I woke up in the split second between the time the gun went off and the time that I was to die. I was sweating and hysterical. I knew the face in my dream. It was my father. That made it even more horrible.

My mother and father both heard my scream and came running into my room. I only wanted my mother's comfort. I was exhausted, but too terrified to go back to sleep. I had never had a nightmare before. Unlike most of my dreams, I could remember every detail of it . . . every feeling . . . every sound . . . but I couldn't repeat any of it to my mother. It was too horrid.

The same nightmare recurred several times during the few months that followed. Not until the third or fourth time did I discover that a pattern had been established: the terrible nightmares always occurred on the fifth day of my menstrual cycle, and I had been raped on the fifth day of my cycle. Each succeeding dream was less terrifying than the previous one, and almost as soon as I discovered the pattern, the dreams ceased.

Until the nightmares, I had convinced myself I was through with the rape. Even after my father's emotional outburst, I had tried to go on with my life as if the rape had never happened.

Since the court proceedings were over, I figured I should be finished with it all. I had set up a type of bargain. By not talking about it, I would not have to experience the pain: my own pain, Dave's pain, my parents' pain. Another result of the bargain was that because I wasn't talking about it, they weren't either. We all played a little game of pretending that it never happened. For a while it worked, but eventually my denial gave way to depression.

The first indication that something was still wrong came with the first nightmare. Shortly after that Dave and I returned to college. We saw each other every day, and almost that often I was given assurances that his love for me had not changed. Yet I knew something was wrong. The following is from a letter I sent across campus to him soon after we returned to school in September.

> I'm getting so used to hearing you tell me that you love me, that I feel like it's just the convenient thing to say. I know you mean it when you say it, but. . . .

I knew it in my head, but I was beginning to have trouble *feeling* his love for me in my heart. I went on in the letter to ask him if he would call me more often or send me notes. I had begun to feel less and less special to Dave. I needed to have him tell me constantly and in many different ways that he still cared about me. These feelings were a result of my beginning to face up to my pain. I had been violated. A stranger off the street had held the power to steal away my dignity, my significance. I was beginning to *feel* that, and it showed up in my relationship with Dave. In a note to him, I wrote:

> I don't want you to feel like you have to spend money on me . . . one dandelion that would remain in a vase until it was totally wilted and then would go in a scrapbook to remind me in future days that, one day in the past, Dave made an ordinary day special

by going out of his way to make a girl feel like a princess again. I guess I just want to feel like that special person to you that you tell me that I am.

From deep inside the feelings of dirtiness and ugliness and worthlessness had finally begun to surface. As a result, I desperately wanted to feel like a beautiful princess deserving of all the attention of a court of attendants.

Dave did try to make me feel special. I'll never forget the time he and a friend came to my dorm and surprised me with a huge arrangement of flowers. They had been out in the country on his friend's motorcycle and had come across an elderly woman selling flowers from her garden. Dave rode all the way back on the cycle holding a five-pound coffee can full to overflowing with the home-grown flowers. It was the most beautiful assortment I had ever seen, and I will always remember how very special it made me feel.

But in spite of all Dave's attention, I was unable to keep the mountain of negative emotions from overshadowing whatever brief moments of joy I had. I fell deeper and deeper into depression, becoming two different emotional beings. I was either extremely high or extremely low, unable to find a medium level of stability.

My highs were unhealthy bursts of energy. At times I was ridiculously silly and turned into the hall clown in our dorm. I was the source of many a laugh as I would sneak into a friend's room to sew her pant legs together, put cornflakes in her bed, glue her shoes to the floor, or blitz the entire room with toilet paper. Everyone around me was having a good time, and although I was the source of their fun, inside I ached. The laughing hurt, and I was alone.

My lows were dangerously low. I would become so depressed that I was almost in a trance. Often I would sit in the cold, open stairway of the dorm with my guitar and sing sad songs, wallowing in the emptiness of the echo that came from my hollow surroundings. If the songs weren't sad enough, I would write songs that were. If I was not singing, I was quiet and alone with my thoughts. I did not think about the rape during these times. Instead, I fantasized more pain—imagining Dave leaving me or someone I loved being killed. My grades began to reflect these lows as I cut classes to sit alone in a cold corner or walk the campus in silence.

My dates with Dave were often a combination of these highs and lows. He could never predict when his seemingly carefree, fun-loving date would suddenly lapse into a state of depression. I can only imagine how helpless he must have felt as he watched my moods fluctuate during those times. I was riding an emotional roller coaster; while at the top I found escape from the pain at the bottom. As time passed, the gap between my highs and lows would narrow. But before that could happen, I was to hit rock-bottom.

> O God, my God, why have you gone from me,
> Far from my prayers, far from my cry?
> To you I call, and you never answer me;
> You send no comfort, and I don't know why.
>
> Into your hands I commend my spirit, O Lord;
> Into your hands I commend my heart,
> For I must die to myself in loving you;
> Into your hands I commend my love.

I was praying this song as I sat on the inside back stairway of the three-story brick dorm and sang with my guitar . . . calling out to my God, the God who had called me to serve Him in the city—that awful, dirty, horrible city that had swallowed me and spit me back out again to walk the earth a beaten creature. The steps were hard and cold, as hard and cold as the depths I was reaching as I poured out these words with voice and tears.

You've been my guide since I was very young;
You showed the way when I needed someone's hand.
And now I'm lonely; nobody's by my side;
Stay near, my Lord, and be my friend.

Despite my despair, I was very aware of God's presence as I sang. He was the only one who really knew what I was feeling. He could see the aching hole inside me—the emptiness that no one else could see. Even though I couldn't believe that void would ever go away, it was a comfort to know that He knew my pain.

But, God, how can You be the same God to whom I committed my life, the same God who loved and cared for me in the past? I know You're there, God, but how could You leave me so alone? I sang, searching for answers I could not find. Was there no one who could take that emptiness from me? Often I would start out singing in anger, "O God, my God, why have you gone from me? You send no comfort, and I don't know why." I would sing it over and over and over again until my anger turned to a quiet, almost peaceful sadness.

I was singing to God, but I did not feel close to Him. He was somewhere way off in the distance, hearing me, watching me, but, for some cruel reason unknown to me, choosing not to come close to me—to give me answers. I was alone and would always be . . . alone.

O Lord,
How can I give of myself when I can no longer believe in myself?
How can I love when I cannot give of myself?
How can I trust when You send no comfort in the blackest night?
You say that You open doors, yet I cannot find these doors.
I am caught in a giant web. I cannot see my foe.
What is it that has caught me in its web?
Is it circumstance or tragic fate?
Is it You, God?
Or another person?
Who has done me wrong?

And, oh, Lord, how do I get out?
My arms are outstretched. I cry aloud.
Yet, no one hears.
The deadening silence is driven into my head,
And back out again.
Thundering, throbbing.
Why? Why?
Where is the answer?
O Lord, shine a light, for I need it.
Give me hope and strength,
For I am weak and ready to fall.
Don't let me fall, O Lord.
Don't let me fall.

Oh, help.

I wrote the following letter to God in October, 1969.

Why Lord, why?

I can't take this life. It's too much for me. I have asked you many times for help, but I can't ever find it. I'm weak, Lord. I'm not who I was. I used to be so happy with life—it used to excite me when I would see someone else smile. Now I don't care, no one is smiling anymore. Nothing is beautiful. All is ugly. I try, Lord. I try to forget, but it haunts me. I can't forget it and I can't accept it. It haunts me. It is tearing me apart. I need help. I ask for it, but no one speaks—everything is silent. I can't stand the silence. It's driving me crazy. All communication is lost. People are not people. They are inhabitants of this same lonely world that I walk in but can't live in. Oh, God, where is thy strength?

I want to leave this life—I want to die. A bottle of aspirin—a knife in the chest—Oh, God, it would be so easy for me to do it now. Whence cometh my help?

I want to be myself again. I want so much to be happy and make others happy. But I need help and I'm not finding it.

Every face is a brick wall that says "be happy," huh—"be happy—be happy—what's wrong? What's wrong?" For God's sake everyone knows what's wrong. Why can't somebody help me?

Let's talk about it—oh, God, what good can it do? Who can help—can anyone?

I loved a man and he loved me—but how can he love a nothing anymore? He is losing out. I am pulling him down. Lord, my whole personage has changed. What's the matter? —What's the matter? The word is despair, Lord. I'm giving up—but you can't give up— but you can't go on—but you can't give up—but you can't go on.

How can I be a witness for Christ when I can't feel His strength when I need it?

And oh, God, why won't you ever let me cry when I need to?

If I really loved Dave I would leave him because I am making his life ugly with my sorrows. I am burdening him with my grief and it hurts me to see him burdened. Yet I keep doing it. Oh, God, how bad?

I want to run away—but I can't go home—everything stares me straight in the face there. It's worse there. I can't go anywhere, Lord—It's something I can't shake. It follows me everywhere. There's no out. Oh, God, get me out. Get me out. I can't take it anymore.

Where is all the love you promised me?

I am looking at a plastic world. I try to smile at the people but their faces are plastered stuck. There is no response to my plea for help. Everything is a brick wall. A brick wall—a brick wall and my head hurts from beating against it—my head hurts—everything hurts—it hurts, oh help.

When I first read my suicide letter to God, ten years after I had written it, I was most appalled by the fact that I had even considered killing myself with a knife. It was a solemn reminder of how deeply I had hurt; an actual blade in the chest could not have equaled the intensity of the pain which I had been experiencing. Seeing the letter in my own handwriting made it all too real. This person, so alone and so forsaken that she wanted to die, was me. Me!

During my deepest depression over the rape, I talked with many people. In addition to Dave, my roommate, and other friends in the dorm, I also spoke once or twice with my college chaplain. They all listened and tried to reach out to me, but I still felt alone in the world. I needed them to care for me, but more than anything else I needed them to understand my anguish, my pain. No one understood.

Often during that time I wished I could talk to another rape victim, just to know that someone else in the world knew how horrible rape could be. In recent years I have talked with many victims of rape. Strongly believing that each person's pain is as individual as that person, I will never say, "I know how you feel." Yet it does help to talk with someone who has experienced the same level of pain—such as one rape victim can do with another, or one widow with another, or one paraplegic with another. And fortunately today there are countless Crisis Centers where trained listeners offer valuable information and support.

But back then I knew of no one who could share, either from special training or from personal experience, what I would call my level of suffering. Because I felt so alone, I felt separated . . . no longer a part of the world around me.

The horrible night which follows is vivid in my memory. It occurred within days of the writing of the suicide letter. . . .

Three o'clock in the morning and I was still awake. Kim, my roommate, had been sleeping for several hours. I was alert and very aware of one particular object in the dark room in which I lay . . . a large bottle of aspirin. It wasn't even mine. Kim had been downtown that day and had brought back several items from the drugstore, one of which was a bottle of those little, white pain-killing tablets. That's what I needed. Something to stop the hurt.

As I lay there with my eyes wide-open in the quiet darkness, the bottle became more and more obvious to me, as if it was the only object in a totally evacuated room. I could almost hear it call to me. . . . "Come and get me. I will kill your pain."

I had thought about how I might kill myself for several days. This way, if I took the pills and just got quietly back into bed, no one would know what I had done until morning. By then it would all be over. My only concern was that Kim would be the one to find me. How traumatic that would be for her. But it would have to be this way. Any other way would be so gruesome.

I slipped out of bed quietly, so I wouldn't disturb Kim, and carefully picked up the bottle of aspirin and a glass. The dimly lit hallway was deserted. As I pushed open the door to the bathroom, I was nearly blinded by the bright lights inside. I sat down on the cold tile floor with my back against the wall and stared at the bottle in my hand.

O God, I am sinking. The weight is carrying me down. I can't hold myself up any longer. It's too much, Lord . . . too much. O God, why?

Why? How could You let this happen to me when I gave up my summer to serve You? What about all the slutty, sinful people on this earth? It should have been them, not me. I never deserved that. My standards for living have always been high. I have not only been good, I have served You, God. How could You let this happen to me? Why, God? Why me?

The tone of my supplication was not angry as it may sound, but low and desperate. I felt forsaken and unloved. And if God Himself had forsaken me, who on earth would care for me? Still, the "Why?" surfaced above all the other questions.

I can't explain why I never opened that bottle. Even though I hated God, He still was God, and I never doubted His existence. I only wondered what kind of a monster He could be. He had been real to me in the past. He was real to me at that moment, though I despised Him for the cruelty He displayed by allowing me to suffer so.

I guess I believed that if I killed myself, I would go straight to hell. There would be no time for forgiveness. But that in itself did not scare me. I couldn't imagine that hell could be worse than what I was living then. What bothered me was that I would never know *why* God had let it happen. Why? That one-word question haunted me enough to leave a reason for living just a little longer. I went back to bed as the sun was rising.

10

If only someone could have assured me, "It won't last forever. You'll get over it."

I did not tell anyone about the night I nearly took my own life until several weeks later, not even Dave. Somehow, I was able to find ways to make each day lead to the next, and the weeks passed. My periods of lowest depression over the rape became less and less frequent, and gradually I was able to resume normal activities. Though I still occasionally cut classes, I was able to handle almost a full schedule again by mid-November. I spent less time alone and more time with my friends and with Dave.

All along, Dave had tried very hard to keep me going. He had shared in many of my lowest moments and had been the vehicle of strength and hope through which God had come to me time after time. But I didn't see God at work then. I only saw Dave. He became my knight in shining armor, my white knight, as I called him. I adored him.

More than anything else, Dave and I enjoyed taking long walks together. Often on a Friday night we would walk downtown or to the park near the college. On one particularly chilly November night we decided to brave the cold and walk to the track where Dave had run many meets the spring before. We sat down on the hard bleachers, staring at the deserted field in silence. A pleasant silence. We were together, really together.

"Dave, do you ever wonder what it will be like five or ten years from now?"

"What do you mean?"

"Oh, I mean do you think we'll be together then?"

"Oh, probably. We'll probably be married and have sixteen kids."

"Good grief! I hope not. Two or three would be plenty. . . . Do you ever think about that, Dave?"

"About what?"

"About being married and having kids?"

"Oh, I suppose, once in a while."

"You do?"

"Sometimes, I guess, but mostly I just think about you."

"About me? What do you think about when you think about me?"

"Oh, mostly about loving you."

I responded with an impish smile, jumped up and bounded to the top of the bleachers. "Would you follow me anywhere?" I yelled down to him.

"What are you doing?"

"Do you love me?" I yelled, choking back a giggle.

"Of course I love you, you flake."

"Then would you follow me anywhere?"

"That's a dumb question. What are you doing up there?"

"I'm waiting for you to come love me up here."

"You're crazy!" With that he leaped up and chased after me.

As he ran up diagonally in one direction, I fled down the other side. I reached the ground first and tore off around the track. Dave was not far behind when he stopped and called out to me.

"I'll give you a quarter of a lap head start, and I'll still catch up with you."

"No, you won't! You'll have to hop a plane to catch me."

I had run about three-quarters of the way around the track when I could feel his feet pounding the asphalt behind me. I turned my head just briefly to see where he was and then kicked out a burst of speed. But Dave had a kick left, too. I should have known that from watching him run races on this track. I felt his hand on my neck and immediately surrendered, slowing down to a walk.

"I won!" I hollered, puffing and panting.

"You did not!" Dave laughed, not in the least short-winded.

"I did so . . . I got you, didn't I?"

I fell to the ground, lying on my back with my arms and legs outstretched. I stared up into the sky, laughter dancing in my eyes.

Dave stood directly above me, no longer laughing. He looked down at me intently. "You're so beautiful, Deborah."

I knew how to respond when he called me Deborah. I knew what he was thinking, what he was feeling. I felt it, too. He leaned down and tenderly kissed my cheek, my neck, my lips.

"Let's go," he said softly.

"Where?"

"Back to my room. Greg's gone home for the weekend."

He stood up, extending both hands toward me. I placed my hands in his. As he gently pulled me up, he put his arms around me and our lips met again. If only the walk back to his dorm wasn't so long, I thought to myself.

When we returned to campus, I was glad there weren't a lot of people around. I didn't want to share my world with anyone but Dave that night, not even to say hi. It was warm and quiet inside Dave's room. While I fastened the door and closed the curtains, he lit two candles and put on our favorite Simon and Garfunkel record. As we held each other in that still moment, our passion radiated through one another.

Dave had not touched me since the rape. His touch felt wonderful. His touch felt wretched. I was torn. My feelings . . . a mass of confusion.

"Dave—"

"Oh, Debbie, you feel so good."

"Oh, Dave, I . . . love being here with you." *No, I don't. I don't think I even like it. Why do I feel so dirty?* "We better go, Dave. What if Greg comes back?"

"Don't be silly. I told you. He's gone for the weekend."

"But . . . we better go. . . . It's . . . getting late."

"Debbie, what's wrong?"

"I don't know. I just want to go. Will you walk me back?"

"But Debbie—"

"Please, David, please walk me back now."

It was only two blocks to my dorm. A short, quiet walk. I went straight to my room, grabbed my john pail and a towel, and headed for the bathroom. Why did I feel like this? Ashamed. We hadn't done anything wrong. We weren't going to do anything wrong. We were just enjoying each other. So why did I feel so filthy? I took the shower at the end of the row. No one was there—near the showers. So why did I feel so self-conscious about undressing?

As I stepped into the shower, I became very aware of my breasts. *Don't look at them. They're ugly. I wish they weren't a part of me at all. O God, what's wrong with me?* I put soap all over me. But it wasn't enough. More soap. *I can't get clean. How ugly! How dirty!* I stood in the shower for what must have been twenty minutes trying desperately to get clean. *I must get rid of those dirty hands yanking off my bra, feeling all over me. Dirty, dirty hands. Get your hands off me. They're my breasts. This is my body. You can't have it. Nobody can. Leave me alone. Don't touch me. Don't touch me. I can't stand to be touched. Dirty hands. Dirty hands. Let me up. Get off me. I will never be clean. Dirty, dirty hands. I can't get those awful hands off me. Get them off. O God, get them off!*

I didn't know why I felt that way or what was happening to me. No one had ever said to me, "Don't worry if at times you feel dirty. It's a natural feeling after you've been raped." Oh, if someone had only told me, "It's okay. It's just part of adjusting to a rape." If only someone could have assured me, "It won't last forever. You'll get over it." If only someone had told me . . . if only someone knew . . . if only someone. . . .

11

Then I found strength, self-
confidence, dignity, and hope.

As the weeks passed, Dave and I did discover the beauty of romance in our relationship. Although gradually I was able to find pleasure in our physical attraction to each other, the sentimentalism surrounding our first Christmas together made the sexual aspect of our relationship seem almost unimportant by comparison.

After spending Christmas Eve and Christmas day at home with my own family, I eagerly drove the seventy-five miles to Dave's house to spend a portion of the Christmas vacation with him. The twenty-seventh of December, 1969, was a special night that I will never allow to slip from my memory.

Dave and I had enjoyed a fireside dinner at a restaurant more elegant than was our custom. Upon returning home, we slipped quietly in the back door of his folks' house and down the stairs to the family room. There we savored every moment we had spent together that evening . . . the taste of fine food, the sweet perfume of roses in a silver vase, the glow of soft candlelight reflected in each other's eyes. . . .

"Thank you, David. This has been the most beautiful evening of my life."

"The most beautiful? Of your life?"

"Yes, I can honestly say that."

"Good, because there's more."

"More?"

"Yes, I have something I want to give you." He reached in his pocket and pulled out a small gray box. As he handed it to me, he whispered, "With all my love."

Thirteen pearls surrounded a crest, a diamond in its center. His fraternity pin. My eyes blurred with tears.

"David, I . . . I don't know what to say . . . I—"

"Just say you'll wear it."

"Of course I'll wear it." I threw my arms around him and began to cry.

"All right. All right. Enough blubbering. I've been practicing on the curtains all day. Let me see if I can pin this thing on you."

It was our first commitment to each other. I could hardly wait to get back to school to share our good news with our friends. My roommate's screams, when she first noticed Dave's pin, brought several other friends out of their rooms. The news spread down the hall like a row of toppling dominoes.

Even the guys were excited for us. Two nights after we got back to school, Dave's fraternity brothers held a pinning ceremony. Dave and I stood outside the front door of my dorm as forty male voices serenaded us in three-part harmony. At the end of the ceremony, the president of the fraternity offered his good wishes and presented me with a bouquet of long-stemmed, pearl-white roses. I felt like a queen with a court full of attendants, my knight at my side.

This was the first identifiable turning point in my life after the rape. I was beginning to believe in Dave's love for me, to feel it as well as know it, and with this I regained some of my self-respect and a sense of control over my own life. Yet, I was still in constant need of reassurances, feeling insecure and inadequate much of the time.

Another turning point occurred in the spring of that same year, my sophomore year. With the help of my friend Karen, I was able to regain the self-confidence I had not known since before the rape.

I was sitting alone at my desk when I heard a knock at the door. It was Karen, one of my newer friends, looking very serious. Even though we hadn't known each other long, I knew it was not like her to wear such a grave expression. In cloak-and-dagger manner she looked back around into the hall, then entered, closing the door behind her. As she spoke, she barely whispered.

"Now, Debbie, I could really get into trouble for talking to you like this. It's about the Beta Chis. We had a meeting tonight after the tea, and a lot of us were really disappointed that you didn't show up tonight. Somebody said you went to the Gamma Nu event because you didn't think you could make it into the Betas."

I had not gone through sorority rush as a freshman, but had decided to wait and rush as a sophomore. And what Karen said was true, although I was shocked that she was saying all this to me. In the first place, if I was a naïve goody-two-shoes, Karen invented the term. She was straighter than anyone I had ever met. And what she was doing was strictly against all rules of sorority rush; the entire sorority could get fined for it. It was called "dirty rushing."

"I can't actually guarantee you a bid, but I'm willing to bet that you'll be voted in if you go to our last tea on Friday."

On our campus there were five local sororities, none of which held any national affiliation. The procedure was to attend all the sororities' events at the beginning of rush and then gradually narrow to one at the very end. I had narrowed my choice to two, Gamma Nu and Beta Chi. Afraid that the Betas would not accept me, my final choice had been the Gamma Nus, a group of humanitarian-type girls who were mainly concerned with societal and environmental issues. Although all the sororities had many attractive girls, Beta Chi was stereotyped as the beauty-queen sorority. They always had more representatives on the homecoming court than any of the others. They were also known to win the academic trophy fairly regularly, as they managed to keep their grade points high. This was the sorority to which Karen belonged. This was the sorority that wanted me as a member? I couldn't believe it!

I pictured in my mind the actives I knew and those whom I

had just recently met. . . . Mary Jo was an attractive, brilliant student. Andrea, tall and thin, was beautiful enough to be a model. Barbie, a vivacious, active cheerleader, had been on the homecoming court for the second time this year. Every girl I thought of had so much going for her . . . good looks, talent, popularity, intelligence. And these were the girls who wanted me to join them, who felt I belonged? Karen was telling me so. Was it really true? Me? A rape victim, who out of total despair had nearly committed suicide just a few short months ago?

At that moment, Karen, unknowingly, had handed me the biggest vote of confidence possible. An attractive, intelligent, talented coed was telling me that's what *I* was. After all I had been through, I had been unable to see myself as anything but degraded, unwhole, dirty, and abused.

"It's your decision now. I've done what I felt I had to do." With that she left.

I held up my small hand mirror and stared at myself for a long time. My contacts made my eyes look even bluer than they naturally were. My long, dark blond hair was shiny and soft; my chubby-cheeked, baby-faced smile looked more womanly now. I was beginning to feel pretty, something I had not felt in nearly a year.

But more than that, I sensed something wonderful, really wonderful, rising up from deep inside of me. It made me want to run through a daisy field . . . hold my arms outstretched, look straight up into the blue sky, and turn around and around and around, breathing in the freshness of the air and drinking in every marvelous sensation surrounding me. . . . *I am a beautiful person again. I now can believe . . . I truly am . . . beautiful!*

At first, joining a sorority had not been all that important to me. I had decided to go through rush just for the fun of meeting new people. But I'm convinced that Karen's "dirty rush" and my ultimate acceptance as a Beta Chi helped immensely in my being able to go on with my life and move toward eventual acceptance of the rape. Dave had been telling me all along that I was special, but somehow I almost came to expect and even demand that from him. Not until I was able to see that other people also thought of me this way was I able to recover my image of self-worth that had been lost at the time of the rape.

Other incidents also contributed to the rebuilding of my self-esteem. I was asked to sing and play my guitar in the Peanut Pit, a coffeehouse on campus, where I was well-received and asked back often. I not only heard, but inhaled every bit of applause offered. I also played guitar and led singing every Sunday evening for a high school youth group at one of the churches in town. Not only did I feel accepted there, but also needed and wanted. By the time I was a junior, my grades had moved from my lowest 1.7 semester to a 3.6 on a 4.0 scale. I had become very involved in my education classes and felt important, and again, needed in the second-grade class where I helped with reading. At the end of my junior year, I was voted a semi-finalist for May Day Queen.

In themselves, none of these events would have been enough to bring healing, but when I put them all together, I could see a progression taking place. God was continually using the people around me to help in the rebuilding of my life. Day by day my self-respect was returning, my self-confidence was growing, and my self-worth as a vital, contributing person was surfacing to a point where even I could see it. I needed these affirming experiences. Some of them were bestowed upon me; others I sought myself. In combination, they helped to gradually lift me out of my periods of depression.

It was the beginning of my acceptance of the rape, but only a beginning. Other people had contributed toward the healing process, but further restoration would have to take place without their help. Together, Dave and I would have to face more pain.

12

No, God, not now.
I don't want to hurt now.

I spent the summer following my sophomore year at our church camp as a full-time staff counselor. It was a rewarding time for me, and I experienced incredible personal and spiritual growth living in that environment. But when September drew near, I was anxious to return to school and Dave.

After a summer of having to drive two hours just to see each other, it was good to be together again. During the year-and-a-half Dave and I had been dating, we had done a lot of talking, and we had a favorite place in which to do it. There was a grade school not far from campus, and our special spot for problem-solving was at the end of the slide on the playground. Warm weather or cold, we would go there to make decisions or simply to be alone to share each other's day. We would reminisce about the good times we had spent together and dream about our future.

On our second night back at school, we returned there for a "slide talk." Dave sat down first at the end of the slide as he always did and then pulled me down in front of him, his arms around my waist. Relaxed and content, I laid my head on his shoulder.

"Doesn't it feel good to be back?" I asked.

"Sure does."

"It's almost like coming home to our home, isn't it?"

"Yes, Debbie. We've built a lot of memories in this town."

"Not all of them good ones."

"No, but we've come out of it all loving each other an awful lot. And we've had our share of fun times, too."

"Like the time I planted clues all over town for you to follow to find your birthday present?"

"I still can't believe you put that one in the fish pond in the park. . . . Deborah . . . I . . . let's walk." We walked. First just outside of the playground and then around the block. I knew Dave had something on his mind; he had called me Deborah. We came back to the slide, and he sat down and looked up at me. The expression on his face was difficult to interpret. I had not seen this one before.

I extended my hands to him and knelt down in front of him. "David, what is it?"

"Deborah, I want you to be my wife."

"Oh, David, I want to be your wife."

Though to anyone else it may have appeared an unromantic setting for a proposal, for us there was no more fitting place. Here we had learned to communicate and solve problems together. Here the foundation of our relationship had been laid. And now here it was that our life commitment to each other had first been spoken.

These same words became the first two lines of our marriage vows exchanged a year later in August of 1971. We knew our first year of marriage would be difficult. We both had a year of school left before we would graduate. I would be doing my student teaching. Dave had some tough classes coming up and had been elected president of the student council which would involve a great deal of time and responsibility. But we were ready for marriage; we were deeply in love and solidly committed to each other.

With the blessing of both Dave's and my parents, we began making wedding plans even before Christmas. My mother and I finalized the details as our special day approached.

Dave called me at home on the morning of our wedding, but we held to our promise to not see each other until the ceremony. Eventually, the moment came. Dressed in my white, Juliet-styled, floor-length wedding gown, I walked to the back of the long aisle and took my father's arm. Dave and his groomsmen were already standing at the front of the sanctuary. Our eyes met. I could not hold back the tears. I fought them the full length of the procession down the aisle. As I approached Dave, I could see that this special moment had brought tears to his eyes as well.

The promises we made to each other and to God in front of our families and friends were of primary significance, and we have repeated our wedding vows to each other each year on our anniversary to refresh and renew the commitment that binds us. But the moment that speaks of the love God gave us to share for a lifetime was the moment in which we first saw each other, the moment in which I walked down the aisle toward Dave to join my life with his. It was a moment of purity, of magnificence. At that moment the gift of a new life was given . . . and received.

In this spirit our lives were joined. In this spirit we celebrated our union with friends and family at our reception. And in this spirit we came together on our wedding night, that moment for which it seemed we had waited forever.

We laid in bed together, realizing how much we belonged together, how right it felt to be naked and held so closely. But as Dave entered me, I felt pain, physical pain. . . . *No, God, not now. I don't want to hurt now. I thought it was supposed to feel good.*

The look on Dave's face revealed how wonderful it was for him. The joy of actually being inside of me for the first time radiated from him. I began to loosen up and the pain lessened. *But, God, this isn't the first time I have hurt like this, is it? Roger Gray hurt me like this.*

Dave's words blocked out these thoughts as he spoke. "Deborah, I love you so much."

"Oh, David, you know I love you. We're really married now, aren't we? This is really all happening, isn't it?"

"Yes, Deborah . . . it's really all happening."

Roger Gray was in my thoughts only briefly that night, but he was there long enough to change my mood from excited expectation to daylight reality. I delighted in pleasing Dave. And I was glad we had saved ourselves for each other on our wedding night. That much about it felt right and good. But my thoughts of Roger Gray tarnished my own long-awaited pleasure.

Dave thought about the rape that night too, but I didn't know it. Not until years later when I sat down to write about it did we discover what each of us was thinking that night. Dave said that he hadn't known what to expect from me the first time we had intercourse. He had even been afraid I might become hysterical.

Discovering each other's memories of that night was a somber realization for us both. We felt deeply saddened that we had to take more to bed with us on our wedding night . . . more than just each other.

13

My hope comes in knowing that
though the past cannot be erased, it
can be dealt with, and lived with,
and then left behind.

Dave and I had spent a great deal of time together before we were married. As with any other couple, a fair amount of that time involved a physical expression of our love for each other, and most of it had been pleasurable for both of us. It had been difficult to save the physical union for our wedding night. We had fought the temptation many times.

The strong physical attraction we shared made it easy for me to deny my thoughts about the rape throughout our honeymoon and well into the early days of our love-making as husband and wife. However, in time my rape experience surfaced again in light of the new dimension in our relationship. When it happened, it came as a shock to both of us. Although we knew it would take time to become completely compatible, we found pleasure in our love-making.

We delighted in being married, in living together. Our first apartment was tiny, but it was *our* home. We had rented a two-bedroom apartment. One bedroom was only large enough to be used as a study; in the other we slept . . . we made love. . . .

"Oh, Dave, will I ever get used to having you as my husband? It's like a dream. I hope I never wake up."

"You mean you're not sick of me yet?"

"Sick of you? It hasn't even been two months. Besides, how could I ever be sick of you? Look at you, you hunk. I want to stay here in bed with you forever."

"Oh, Deborah, it's so sensuous to be in the dark, just feeling you, loving you. . . ."

That night—that moment, so very suddenly, something happened. Terror arose within me. I couldn't suppress it.

"It's awfully dark in here, Dave. I can't see you."

"That's okay. Just hold me."

"I can't see your face." I could not control the horrible

cinema of thoughts racing through my head. . . . *I want to see your face. Turn the light on please. I have to see you. I have to know it's you. I can feel that it's you. It's your voice I hear, but I can't see you. Oh, please, turn on the light. Stop it! Don't come in me! Dave, it's you, isn't it? I know it is. But I can't see you. I have to be able to see you!*

"What's the matter?"

"Nothing."

"You're crying."

"I can't see you, Dave. I know it's you, but I can't see your face. Please come out of me. Stop. Leave me alone. I can't. I can't."

He got up, turned the hall light on, flung the sheet over me, and went into the bathroom. I was left alone with my tears, my pain. I had driven the man I loved from my bed, because I couldn't see his face. Robbed of just one of my senses, all others were captured by fear.

Hearing my sobbing, Dave briskly returned to the bedroom.

"Get ahold of yourself!" He was yelling at me. I had become hysterical.

"I can't."

"Look at me. I'm your husband."

"I know . . . I can't."

"Stop it. You're out of control. Come back to me. I'm your husband. I love you."

"I can't . . . I can't."

"You can. You can. You can." He was shaking me by my shoulders. My head fell back, loosely resting on the tear-soaked sheet. I lay flat. Naked. Weak. The tears still streamed down my cheeks, but no strength was left to energize the sobbing. I became silent, still.

Dave lay next to me, staring at the ceiling. I wanted to

120

reach for him, but I couldn't. I lay limp. Together we lay in silence, desperate to leave the moment behind us, but unable to get up.

He knew what had happened. I knew that he did. I felt my own pain coupled with that which I had inflicted upon him. Again I had forced him to suffer with me . . . this time, intimately.

This was the first time the rape had affected our love-making, but there would be others. I discovered that I had suppressed a mountain of emotions regarding this thing called intercourse. The rape still had its hold on me. No longer able to fool myself or Dave, I realized that I had been unable to give myself completely to him.

I would start out uncontrollably turned-on. *Touch me, Dave, please touch me. . . . But, Dave, I don't want to touch you. Not there. I will touch you anywhere, but don't make me touch that part of you. I don't even want to see that part of you. It's ugly. Don't make me look, and please don't put my hand there. I know it makes you feel good. I want to make you feel good. I want to give you the beautiful feelings you give me. I can't. I love you. I want you. I need you. But not that part of you. Oh, couldn't we just make love without that part? Just let me hold you . . . kiss you . . . feel you close to me.*

Oh, God, will it ever be right? Can I ever love all of you, Dave? I will try to make you believe I do. I don't want to hurt you. I don't want you to know that I just can't accept all of you. I will touch you there. But, please, get it over with. I don't like it. Will I ever like it? Will your penis always be something to get in the way of my enjoyment of you?

It's ugly like Roger Gray's. I never looked at his. His hurt me and left me devastated . . . violated. His stole dignity and wholeness and womanhood from me. And this thing that's attached to you, Dave. I know it's not his, but it's just like his. How can this ever be beautiful? How can this ever be right? Isn't there any other way to make love? Can't we make love without it? Why does it have to be this part of you that makes you feel so good, gives you such pleasure? And why do I have to be a part of that? Why do I have to be the one to make that happen for you?

Will I never have a real orgasm? Will I never know how it's supposed to be . . . how it is for everyone else? We're newlyweds. It's supposed to be so wonderful. Oh, God, for me it has become the hardest part of being married.

I'm okay. Yes, I want you. I know I'm crying. I'm really all right. Don't stop. I'm just letting some feelings out. It's okay. I want you to feel good. I want you to go off. I want to give you that much. Please. I want you to go now. Oh, God, I want this to be over. I love you, Dave, but I can't show you the way I'm supposed to. I can't reach the covers. Please cover me up. I don't like being naked. Don't look at me. I want to get cleaned up. I feel so dirty. . . .

Can this ever be the wedding gift God gave us to share? Can it ever be good? Oh, God, will this ever be beautiful for us? Can healing extend far enough to reach into our bedroom? Oh, God, can it?

Looking back on our love-making during the first year of our marriage, I wonder how we ever kept getting back in bed together. The passion of each moment may have started things, but it could only have been our solid commitment to each other that actually brought us through each time during this difficult period of adjustment. It took months for the intensity of the sexual trauma left by the rape to diminish, but it did, gradually, as we continued to give ourselves intimately to each other.

As Dave and I took control over the sexual aspect of the adjustment to my rape, room was left for still another step to be taken in the healing process. Dave and I had come a long way. Yet there was more. Something still had to be resolved between me and my God. This time Dave could not help.

14

Why, God?
Why me?

By the end of our first year of marriage most of my rape experience had been put neatly on a shelf. I felt good about myself, about our marriage, and about life in general. I was my energetic, enthusiastic self again. Most of life was a celebration. Yet now and then an unresolved question surfaced—the question I had asked God three years before on the night I nearly took my own life. The following letter I wrote to God expresses my need for an answer to that question.

Dear God,

Remember me? I'm Deborah. I committed my life to You at a church retreat when I was a sophomore in high school. I stayed close to You through my high school days even when it was tough to be different—to be a teen-ager and a Christian, too.

I chose a Christian college because I wanted You to be in the center of my life even when I moved away from home, from church, and from my Christian friends. At the end of my freshman year in college, I prayed to You, giving myself to You in service. In that prayer I asked You to take my summer and make it Your own. It was by Your leading that I went to the inner city of Chicago to work in Your church. I could have had my old job back at the department store for another summer and made lots more money, but I chose to serve You instead.

What happened? I thought You wanted me there. That was *Your* work I was doing. It was by *Your* leading that I went there. Did You think that it was better for me to be raped and quit my job than to stay there the whole summer and work for You? I don't understand. It doesn't make sense. You don't still punish people today the way You did in the Old Testament times, do You? Jesus changed all that, I thought. You weren't punishing me, were You? I may make mistakes, but so does everybody else. Why should I deserve that? No, I can't believe You were punishing me. Why then?

Am I just an ungrateful, spoiled child? Should I be thankful to You that it was not much worse? I could have been beaten, stabbed, or raped again by all of Roger Gray's friends. I could have even been killed. Should I thank You instead of question You? Maybe I should. But somehow I can't help but wonder why You let any of it happen at all. You could have prevented it. You know I believe in Your miracles.

The words of Psalm 121 are still familiar to me, God. Do you remember how often I read them during my early days in the city? They were a daily comfort to me then . . .

> The Lord is your keeper;
> the Lord is your shade on your right hand.
> The sun shall not smite you by day,
> nor the moon by night.

> The Lord will keep you from all evil;
> he will keep your life.
> The Lord will keep your going out and
> your coming in from this time forth
> and for evermore.

What about that, God? Shouldn't I believe Your promises? I thought I was special to You. Did I read that wrong, or wasn't that a promise from You to protect me?

I just don't understand. Are You a loving God or are You a vengeful God? Did You have a reason for me to be raped? Did You really *want* that to happen to me? What reason could be good enough for that kind of pain? I nearly killed myself over it. Do you remember that?

I was only 19 years old when it happened. God, that's a very young age to have to face that kind of crisis. I didn't even know what the beautiful, loving, sharing kind of sex was supposed to be like when all of a sudden I was violated in an ugly, twisted, sexual way. I was too young for that. I'm still too young to have been through this kind of suffering. All I have been through, Lord! I'm only 22!

I just don't understand. Most of my life has been put back together now. The nightmares have been over for a long time. Dave and I enjoy each other sexually. I no longer go cold on him. I no longer get upset over violent TV shows exploiting rape. I no longer become nervous and paranoid when I find myself involved in a discussion about rape. Actually, I feel pretty together about the whole thing, except for You, God.

I can go about living my life normally now, except sometimes when I'm sitting in church . . . and I hear all those promises, and I am told that You are a compassionate God who not only loves, but also cares for His people. . . I just don't know what to believe. I just don't understand You, God. It doesn't make sense. I just don't understand.

Trying to understand God's will overwhelmed me. My frustration level raised, I finally went to my minister, hoping to find answers to my questions about God. Our conversation in his office helped a great deal, but it wasn't what was said there that ultimately changed my thinking about God. As I was leaving, Reverend Peterson handed me a copy of a sermon he had preached on a previous date dealing with the will of God. The message that came to me through that sermon changed my life completely.

God allows tragedy to take place in the world because He created man with a freedom to choose God's way or Satan's way. Why did God do that? Why did God allow evil to come into the world in the first place? Why did He allow that opportunity to be there? Why didn't He just make us to only love Him and love each other? And I ask . . . what would love be if one was not free to do otherwise? Love would be a hollow, empty experience. . . . God honored you and me by giving us a will. . . . If we could do no other than to love God, that love would be empty, void; our relationship would be nothing.

This explanation made sense to me. This much I could understand. It seemed rather simple. Because God had given me the freedom to choose His way, I had to recognize that He had given all of mankind that same freedom. Some, for whatever reason, would choose evil over good. One of those people was Roger Gray. Very simply, I had become a victim of Roger Gray's wrong choice.

But I still could not understand why He should allow this to happen to me. "But, God, why me?" It was through the same sermon that I found peace about this question.

The question, "How could God allow this to happen?" is best answered when we quit asking questions about God and go to Him in the midst of the tragedy, no matter how great, and trust Him to be the Good Shepherd who does not forsake His own. And it's there in His arms that somehow He brings meaning to us through it.

Several years ago I met a couple, in the first summer charge I had as a young pastor. They had been faithful members of the church until two years before, and I was told by the Council to call on them. They seldom came out of their house, never came to church, and just seemed to be the saddest people around. I went to the home and introduced myself, and they invited me in. Sorrow was written all over their faces.

I said, "I understand you are members of the church, and I am glad about that. I am your pastor for the summer and wanted to get to know you."

The husband said, "Well, you'll never see me in that church." I said, "Oh."

He said, "Yeah, we used to believe that God cared about us, but two years ago we got convinced that He doesn't. We had one son, just one. We loved him, and we raised him, and we gave him everything we knew. We gave him a Christian faith, and he loved God. And one day, coming home from a date, just outside of town, he missed a curve over there and wrapped himself around a tree, and he was killed instantly. Any God that treats me that way, I'll never love, and I'll never sit in His church."

Well, that's a pretty heavy issue for a young seminarian to walk in on. I didn't know what to say, and I just felt their sorrow and their pain and their grief and I didn't say, "I know how you feel," but I did say, "I'm feeling with you." And then it just flashed across my mind, so I shared it.

I said, "You know, God only had one son, just like you. And He willingly gave that son to die so that He could take upon Himself your pain, your sorrow, your shame, and provide an eternal life for your son, as well as yourselves."

And I said, "I don't know if that means anything to you this afternoon, but I share it for what it is."

And they looked at me and said, "We never looked at it that way before."

I said, "God loves you. God hasn't abandoned you. God cares about you."

And the man began to get big tears welling in his eyes, and I said, "Why don't we just ask God to let that love bear upon us right here and right now," and I felt very much alive in God's spirit and with His leading, and I took that heartbroken mother and that bruised, beat-up father in my arms, and I prayed with them, standing in the middle of that living room. I cried with them. And when we opened our eyes after the prayer, the mother was smiling and the father believed. And joy returned.

God was there all the time. They were just not allowing His love to do its great work in their lives. And when they did, it brought meaning to tragedy and hope out of despair. And they were back in church that next Sunday and continued to be there. They have a hope now. They have been comforted.

I can only explain it by saying they allowed God, who took the risk of creating a freedom that would allow for tragedy, to love them in the midst of it. Remember that no matter how tragic or painful the circumstances, no matter how brutally another's will seeks to destroy you or your loved ones, no matter how tragic the results of your own willfulness, remember, God is there, loving, reaching out, and caring for you. And as you allow Him to, you receive His blessing. . . .

What do we do when we don't understand God's answer? Are we to say, "God, You are unjust, maybe not righteous after all"? If we do that, then we remove ourselves from God's care; we wall ourselves out at the time of greatest need. We go through life cursing God and His people, rather than finding healing for our hearts, even if we cannot gain understanding for our heads.

What I can't resolve, I take to God and leave with Him. I trust Him. I trust that He knows best. And if I have been a victim of some horrible evil, then in the midst of that tragic need, I need the Shepherd's care more than any other time.

My eyes blurred with tears as I read that sermon. I was freshly moved by the story I had heard every Easter since I was a young child. In the light of my own suffering and the suffering of that couple, Jesus' death on the cross took on new meaning. God had *willingly* given His only Son to die. How God must have suffered right along with His Son. How He must have grieved with that couple and felt their loss. How He must have suffered with me over the pain of my rape and shared my anguish when I nearly took my life. Through the cross, God entered my pain and made it His own.

I will never understand God, but I can trust Him. I cannot expect to be spared pain and suffering, but I can go to

God in the midst of it and find comfort and love.

Because I can trust Him, I will never again need to ask the question, "Why me?" I am content to know that God's love is sufficient. In this I have found healing, a healing that cannot be found outside of His love.

People have said that being a rape victim must have been harder for me in some ways because I am a Christian. I say to them . . . I may have had hard questions to ask, but the joy in discovering His healing in the midst of such pain is a joy that can only be experienced by one who loves and trusts God. It is only through Him that there is healing. It is only through Him that my burden is lifted. It is only through Him that I find peace.

15

And there is even joy.
For in the rebuilding of our lives
we discover the fullness of
God's love.

During my adjustment to the rape, most of my anger was directed toward God for allowing the rape to happen. Because I blamed God, it was God I needed to forgive. Although God had done nothing wrong, in my mind He had. I had trusted Him enough to serve Him in the city, yet I was convinced He had forsaken me.

With the help of Reverend Peterson's sermon, I was able to return my trust to God, having learned that His grace is greater than any pain we must bear. In order to reach this point, I had to empty myself of anger and resentment, including that which I felt toward Roger Gray.

Although my life was no longer ruled by those emotions, there was still something wrong inside of me . . . something missing. The letter I wrote to Roger Gray (but never actually sent to him) reveals the essence of those feelings.

Roger Gray,

You stole something from me, but I don't know what to call it. You left me with a feeling, a feeling I can't explain.

It's as if when you raped me, you threw me into a deep, dark pit. I emerged naked. Piece by piece, I was able to retrieve my clothing. Sometimes I had to walk great distances to find the pieces, but I did find them. The first item I had to recover was control over my own life. Then I found strength, self-confidence, dignity, and hope. I'm even discovering my own sexuality. I have found peace with my God. Yet, there was nothing I could put on that could make me feel like a complete woman. You must have taken a piece with you, Roger Gray. You see, a part of me was left naked. Inside of me, it felt like a hole, a hole that could never be filled . . . a vital part of me . . . stolen. Will I never be a whole woman?

Why did the rape do this to me? Why do I feel like in that part of me called woman there is a vast emptiness? Roger Gray, I don't know how you accomplished that, but you did. I can look like a woman, I can act like a woman, I can do everything a woman does, but I can't feel like a woman. How did you take that from me, Roger Gray? I don't understand why I'm left with this chasm inside of me. Every other grown female seems like so much more of a woman. Sometimes I even get jealous of other women. They are whole, but I've been robbed. I look in the mirror, but I'm not all there. There's something missing. I can't explain it to anyone else. I don't understand it myself, but it's missing . . . gone . . . stolen. Will I never find it? Must I always live with this hole inside of me? Can I never be a *woman?*

This was the final question. I don't believe I ever expected an answer when I asked it. I had come to accept the fact that the rape would leave me damaged forever in this area of my life. All else had been resolved. But since I had no idea how I might rid myself of that emptiness, I came to believe that it was something I would have to live with indefinitely. How could a person so mutilated ever become entirely whole? I believed it simply could not happen.

Dave and I worked for a year following college graduation to save enough money for him to go to law school. When Dave entered school, I was five months pregnant. The first semester was difficult for both of us. Law school was much tougher than college for Dave, and because the baby was due in January, I was no longer working. We had moved to a new town and were now four hundred miles away from either of our parents. It was a lonely time for us, but I managed to keep busy typing Dave's papers, reading books, crocheting baby things, and getting the little nest ready.

By the time January arrived, I was filled to overflowing with anticipation. I was still a few days away from my due date when I felt my first contraction. It came about six o'clock on a Friday night.

After thirty-six hours of contractions, with four-and-a-half hours of hard labor, Elizabeth Sue Roberts was born, all eight pounds and four ounces of her! I was exhausted, but ecstatic. Our little Beth was laid on a table near enough so I could see her. She was crying up a storm. She had a hematoma on her head, bruises from the forceps, a face as wide as an Eskimo's, hair that stuck straight out, and the wrinkles of a newborn baby monkey. She was beautiful.

She was my child. Dave's child. God's child. A living, moving, breathing, crying, kicking, wonderful baby person. She had come from inside of me . . . me! I was just Deborah Roberts, but that floppy little baby on that table had just emerged from me!

After some minor repair work, I was wheeled back to my room in time to catch about an hour of sleep. When the breakfast trays came around at 7:30 A.M., I was awake. Awake and famished. I refrained from calling Dave at home until about 8:30. Finally, I couldn't wait any longer. I dialed our number, and a very groggy, "What are you doing awake?" came from the other end of the line.

"Why should I be asleep? I just had a baby!" I felt wonderful. My exhaustion could not begin to cloud my excitement. I had never experienced such fullness of joy . . . such appreciation for life—mine, Dave's, and little Beth's.

When the exhilaration of the morning had mellowed in the late afternoon, I still had no desire to sleep. Instead, I had an unrefusable urge to be alone with my thoughts. . . . *I am proud . . . I am beautiful . . . I am grateful . . . I am a mother . . . I am a woman . . . Oh, dear God, I am! I am a woman! I am a whole woman! Look at me now. I am totally free of you, Roger Gray. You no longer have a hold on me. Not even you can take away this moment. Not even you. I am a whole woman!*

Looking back on the birth of our first child evokes many emotions. I marvel at the miracle of life . . . how, by the wonderful grace of God working between man and woman, we are given such an incredible gift as life itself. It's overwhelming.

But for me, this gift meant even more. I would never again feel that emptiness, that hole inside that I had been left with after the rape. The birth of our child meant more than motherhood to me. It meant womanhood. For the first time I *felt* like the woman I was. I find this all very hard to understand. Again I ask, why did the rape make me feel like I had been robbed of my womanhood? And why had the birth of our child changed all that? I don't have an answer to these questions.

And yet, I must ask one more question. What if, because of the rape or for some other reason, I had been unable to have children? Would I never have found that healing? My history with God and the relationship we have had over the years causes me to believe that had I not been able to have children, He would have found another way to provide healing for that emptiness.

God has given me motherhood . . . God has given me womanhood . . . God has given me freedom . . . freedom to enjoy His gifts.

He has given me Dave as a total person and myself as a total person. He has given us our bodies.

There were days when even during our love-making I did not want to be naked. I did not want to see myself or to have Dave see me. Over the years, God has given me mirrors. At first it was difficult. . . .

But, oh, how beautiful it is now to be free to be naked and to enjoy being naked. I am proud of who I am. I am a person who has been raped. Yet, I am a person who has been changed. The sky darkened, the winds came, and my house was blown away. But brick by brick, God and I and Dave have built a new house. And it's stronger and better and more beautiful than the old one could ever have been.

It was dark. I could see out the front window, and the street was quiet. I watched as the last light was turned off in the upstairs window of the house across the street. They were in bed. That's where I wanted to be . . . yet, not to sleep.

The fire was low, its only sound a crackle. Piercing the darkness with its flicker, it fought to stay alive. Dave was stretched out on the floor asleep. Maybe we wouldn't even make it up to the bedroom this time.

Joining him on the floor, I slowly ran my fingers up the back of his leg and moved them toward his hip. I could feel his body stir in response to my invitation. He was not yet awake, yet he was already feeling . . . and I was feeling. Together we would explore each other as if our bodies had never met.

He was awake now. The surprise at finding me unclothed was enough. As I touched him and brought him to me, his fingers began to reach as well. . . .

Together we give. Together we love. Together we enjoy. There are no tears of pain now. Any tears that come are an expression of the overwhelming joy we feel. We come so close to each other that we pass through and share oneness with each other and with God.

It did not happen suddenly. It has taken a long time. But, I have the wings of a butterfly now. I have come from the ground, no longer crawling on the earth. I have grown to full beauty. I am free. I can fly. There is nothing to hold me back, nothing to pull me down. There is nothing I can't do, nothing I can't give. I can live and love in joy . . . in victory. . . . I am free!

Epilogue

Dave went on to finish law school and is now successfully practicing law. During his first year as an attorney, we were again richly blessed, this time with the birth of a son. By the time Beth was five and Jeremy had reached the delightful age of two, I had begun to work on this book. Although Dave supported me in my writing from the beginning, he had decided he did not want to read any of it until it was completed. But one day, not too long after I had begun writing, his curiosity got the best of him.

It was Wednesday. He had slipped out early in the morning, not waking myself or either of the kids. He wanted to get to work early so he could run off copies of my newest material for me before anyone else in his office came to work. I had placed the yellow, legal-sized pages in his briefcase the night before. On top of the pile was the section which I had just finished writing entitled, "The Rape." As he stood in front of the copier, he suddenly realized what he held in his hands. It had been years since we had talked about my rape in detail. His curiosity was too much for him. . . . *How does she handle the description of the rape itself? Did she write it all? Without being too graphic? How detailed is it?* He would take it back to his own office and just take a peek at what was there.

Alone in that small room, crowded with law books, his massive desk smothered in legal publications, files, and paperwork, Dave did not put the pages down until he had read all of it. By the time he called me at home a couple of hours later, he had calmed down some, but was still feeling emotions he hadn't known were there.

Suddenly it had become real to him from an entirely different perspective. At the time that I had been raped, Dave and I had only been dating for four months. We had made no commitment to each other . . . no fraternity pin, no ring. At that time, he didn't feel I was necessarily his. But now we had been married almost eight years. I was his wife, a dearly loved part of him, and Roger Gray had violated that. I could hear the rage singe through the inside of him as he uttered, "It makes me want to find that guy and . . . !"

At first I was confused by the fact that after ten years he still had such anger left. We talked about it after the kids were in bed that night. Not until then did I fully realize that most of what Dave had had to deal with at the time of my rape and soon thereafter was me, not the rape itself. He had spent most of his energies in helping me through it. He had never needed to deal directly with the rape, as I had. The details were not embedded in his mind. Now he was having to look directly at the rape, and it was painful.

In his mind, Dave was having to picture me, as his wife, with Roger Gray French kissing me, squeezing my breasts, dragging me down the grimy stairs, pulling my underpants down, and inserting his ugly self into me. I had lived with the details replaying in my mind a thousand times until it was no longer painful, but just a memory. Dave had not. Now it was my turn to share in Dave's pain, and it hurt us both. We were able to work through it, as this kind of pain was not new to us, but oh, we wanted so desperately to close the door on the rape and leave it all behind.

Dealing with my total rape experience involved passing through a number of stages of emotional adjustment: shock, denial, anger, rationalization (I should be finished with it—let's go on as if it never happened), depression, and acceptance. One of the major points I want to make in this book is that past the acceptance stage, there comes another—the assimilation stage. This is when a rape victim can look herself straight in the eye and say, "I'm healed. I'm whole. I am myself. It's all over. I can go on with my life and leave the whole rape experience behind me completely. It's no longer a problem for me. I don't have to spend any more time with it. It's over." I want so desperately to be able to tell rape victims and those who are trying to understand rape that this is all true—that there is a finality about it. But Dave's experience of reading the rape scene was a sober reminder that that would not be telling the whole truth. I have had to face the fact that the rape is something that will always be a part of me . . . something I cannot shove in the closet and shut the door on forever. A discussion I had with my minister convinced me of this.

It was through Reverend Jennings that I first felt God leading me to write this book. When I decided to do it, I went to him and told him about it, seeking his support. Over the past two years, Reverend Jennings has walked through all of the writing of it with me—reading each draft, offering advice, and helping me keep my perspective. One particular talk that we had in his office lasted nearly two hours. I walked away from that meeting feeling somewhat confident about the road ahead. A couple of hours later, I nearly fell apart. I was confused, hurting, torn—feeling like I would come unglued altogether.

We had talked, among other things, about signals. Most likely Roger Gray had given me some signals that could have clued me as to his intentions, but I missed them. He asked me to go to his party. He followed me across the street. Who knows what else? We came from different backgrounds. We weren't speaking the same language. My sun-streaked hair was long and blowing in the wind. I was a sexual being. I was there alone. I said "Hi." I was sending out some signals as well.

Until this time, I hadn't allowed myself to feel guilt over the rape. I know from a year's experience as a volunteer with a rape crisis team that guilt is a very normal thing for a rape victim to feel whether she "has reason" to feel guilty or not. Now, what I am going to say next is very important: I am not taking any responsibility for the rape itself. I did not deserve to get raped. *No woman does, regardless of the circumstances.* I am merely taking responsibility for the fact that I missed some signals sent out to me and that I sent some signals myself. Taking even this small responsibility made me feel guilty. It shouldn't have, but it did.

A mother sends her child to the store on his bike for a loaf of bread. On the way to the store, the child gets hit by a car. The mother feels guilty. "If I had gone to the store myself, this never would have happened." Maybe the child was riding no-handed in the middle of the street. Maybe the driver of the car ran a red light. It doesn't matter. The mother feels guilty no matter who was ultimately responsible. She shouldn't. She does.

I felt this same kind of guilt. Though it's negative and painful, I think it's normal and healthy. It's an emotion that needs to be vented.

But this by itself was not what made me feel like I was falling apart. I had dealt with a lot more than this in the past. I could handle some guilt. What hurt was that I had convinced myself I had dealt with everything. Suddenly I began to dig into myself. I opened a door and found a skeleton I didn't know existed. I had been building up walls of protection for myself for years. A wall came down, and it hurt.

Although I had been able to say to myself in the past . . . I am healed . . . I am whole, at this point I had to say to myself . . . you still have some healing to do. You have a problem to deal with here. Even though it has been put behind you, right now you hurt over this rape thing. Right now, ten years later.

I want to have it over for good. I don't want it to touch me any more—ever. I can't have that. I want it to be as if it never happened. I can't have that. I want to shut the door on it and never see the door opened again. I can't have that. This is the whole truth that, painfully, I had been hiding from myself.

My hope comes in knowing that though the past cannot be erased, it can be dealt with, and lived with, and then left behind. The past won't go away, but I can be healed. I can be normal. I can be whole. I can be myself. I am a different self than I was before. I have hurt, but I have grown through all my pain. The rape will never be completely gone from me. It will always be a part of me, but that's okay. I can live with that. It won't always hurt me. Only when I dig down deep inside of myself and reach and grab for everything that makes me, me—only then will I have to come face-to-face with that part of me again. And it will hurt, but that's okay, because it is a part of *me*. God did not make me a complicated being so I could be comfortable with myself. He made me the person I am so I can take the whole package—the suffering with the healing, the pain with the joy, the struggle with the peace—and be able to hold it all in my arms and look up at Him and say, "Thank You, God, for life."

Dear World,

Please treat me like the whole person that I am. I laugh over Dr. Seuss stories with my two children, and once in a while I stumble over the words. I love to play racquetball and sometimes I lose. I do needlepoint or crochet in front of the TV and get frustrated when I have to rip out my mistakes. I love to make strawberry and blueberry jam, but I quickly tire of planning suppers. I go camping and hiking, and I can actually enjoy living in a tent for more than a week at a time, as long as the bathrooms have showers.

When I am already late for a dentist appointment and I have to wait for a freight train, I am quick to get uptight. I get depressed over silly little things when it's that time of the month. Injustices like child abuse and indifference to the world's poor upset me. I get teary-eyed at weddings and cry at funerals. I melt like a young lover when my husband picks out a sentimental card for my birthday. I get crabby when he has too many meetings.

I have two children, but I had three pregnancies. One ended in a miscarriage. Just because I suffered a rape does not make me exempt from other trials.

You see, I really am normal. I experience life in many of the same ways other people do. I am no more. I am no less. So please, don't identify me with the rape every time I am low. Other circumstances are now the source of my struggles. And on the other hand, please don't expect me to constantly be on top of the world just because God has brought me through a very deep valley.

In most ways, I am like anyone else. So please don't treat me like I'm dying if the cancer has been cured. And please don't expect me to soar like an eagle if I have the wings of a butterfly.

Debbie

APPENDIX

What Can I Do to Protect Myself From Attack?

Some Startling Facts and Information

What About Medical Help?

Where Should the Victim Go for Help?

What About the Legal Aspects of Rape?

What About Emotional Help?

What Is the Church's Response?

What About Family and Friends?
What Can We Do to Help?

Stages of Adjustment

For ease of reading, the rape victim has been referred to in the feminine gender in this appendix. The material provided may also be applicable to male victims of rape.

The publisher wishes to thank its local rape crisis team, the Rape Crisis Team of Kent County, Michigan, which provided material used in this appendix, with special appreciation to Martha McGavic Barr, D. J. Chivis, and Donna Gutierrez.

What Can I Do to Protect Myself From Attack?

Rape can occur any time, any place to anybody, including the Christian . . . including you. Therefore, it is important to be conscious of situations and habits that can make you a potential rape victim. Practicing preventive measures can reduce your chances of becoming a victim. The following list is not intended to be all inclusive; it is, however, meant to help you become aware of alternative ways to deal with situations that could otherwise leave you vulnerable to attack.

1. *When answering your door* to salesmen, deliverymen, or repairmen, you may wish to call out, "I'll get it, dear," or, during the course of the conversation, you may wish to refer to your sleeping husband in the other room (whether or not he is at home). You may also choose not to answer your door at all. (Most meter readers, for example, will leave a card that you can fill out and return by mail.)

In any case, never admit a stranger without first asking to see an I.D. or company card. If the person at your door is not expected, first call his company and check on him. You may wish to call a neighbor and ask them to be aware of the situation, or you may request that the person at your door come back at a more convenient time. (You can arrange for your husband or a friend to be with you at that later time.) Although this may seem embarrassing or awkward to you at first, you will discover that most legitimate callers will not only be patient, but will mention that *their* wives answer their doors with caution as well.

2. *When out in your car,* always choose well-lighted areas in which to park, and lock your car whenever you leave it, no matter how long you intend to be away. When returning to your car, always check inside before you get in.

Keep your car in good repair and always have at least a quarter of a tank of gas in it. If your car should break down on the highway, raise the hood, then get back into the car, lock the doors, and stay in it if possible. If passing motorists offer to help, ask them if they would call the authorities for you.

3. *If you suspect someone is following you,* proceed cautiously to the nearest location where you are assured of help—for example, a police or fire station. Don't go home. The person may be following you to find out where you live.

4. *When you are walking alone,* walk with a purpose and become well-aware of your surroundings. When you are daydreaming or lost in thought, you become the perfect target for attack. You should be aware of what businesses or homes in your area can offer you safety if necessary. Numerous cities now have organized "neighborhood watch groups" where volunteers are taught to be alert to any suspicious activity in their neighborhood.

Many young mothers feel safe in the company of their own children. However, unless their children are old enough or capable enough to assist them in a threatening situation, they are fooling themselves. Many attackers have been known to rape their victims as the children watch.

Be aware that you do have alternatives, and live your daily life with caution. When you become aware of the situations and habits that can make you a potential rape victim, then you are taking the necessary steps toward protecting yourself.

Unfortunately, whether or not you have taken precautions, an attack can occur. No one can tell you what course of action to take if you are attacked. Only you can decide that.

However, some rapes have been prevented by using different means of escape. Any one of these methods could work, but none are guaranteed to work:

1. Pray out loud.
2. Quote Scripture.

3. Scream (Don't scream "Help!" Scream "Fire!").
4. Fake a seizure.
5. Act crazy or mentally deranged.
6. Tell him it's the wrong time of the month.
7. Put an Alka-Seltzer tablet in your mouth (causes foaming at the mouth).
8. Urinate.
9. Force your finger down your throat to induce vomiting.

Most rapists who have planned their attack may also have anticipated how you may attempt to get away. Trying to escape from him may not be as effective as inventing a way to make yourself repulsive, causing *him* to want to leave *you.*

Each situation is different, so try to remain calm and decide whether it's better to run, scream, fight back, talk, or submit. For example, screaming in an open field most likely will not help and may provoke your assailant.

If you do decide to try to get away, you may be able to use something to help you such as a lighted cigarette, keys carried between fingers in a closed fist, a well-placed kick (groin) or poke (eyes, nose, Adam's apple).

You may wish to carry a bottle of spray (may be commercially prepared or prepared by you, such as a lemon-juice squeeze bottle filled with ammonia), but watch for wind direction or you may end up spraying yourself. Also, remember that an assailant does not usually wait around for the victim to dig in her purse for a weapon, and this type of weapon at best can only provide a brief moment for escape. (Also be aware of the possible dangers of small children getting into these devices.)

Most rapists expect a victim to be passive, so finding a way to throw him off guard momentarily may allow you to get away. But under no circumstances should you do anything to endanger your life, especially if the assailant has a weapon.

Remember, rape is something you can get over. It is not worth your life.

So examine your habits and challenge yourself to change the ones that may make you vulnerable to attack. This is not to say you need to live in fear, but you do owe it to yourself and to those you love to live cautiously. By living in awareness you will greatly reduce your chances of becoming a victim of rape.

Some Startling Facts and Information

- Rape is *not* a sexual act of passion. Rape is a crime of violence and power using sex as the weapon. The rapist chooses to feel powerful by humiliating and degrading his victim.
- Not just young, attractive women are victimized by rapists. Persons of all ages, all physical appearances, all income levels, and all educational backgrounds are victims of sexual assaults. No one is immune. It is not uncommon for men and boys to be sexually assaulted. Ages of reported victims range from infants to people in their nineties.
- Rapists are generally *not* sexually sick, psychotic individuals. Many rapists have access to a willing sexual partner. Sex is not the primary motivation for a rapist. The convicted rapist is found to have a normal sexual personality. He differs from a normal person in having a greater tendency to express violence.
- An unwilling woman can be raped. In at least 85 percent of all rapes, physical force and threats are used. Anyone can become immobilized by fear, verbal threats, or weapons.
- Most women enjoy consensual sexual relationships, but rape is *not* sexual and definitely *not* consensual. Attacks, intimidation, injury, abuse, humiliation, threats, and degradation are *not* enjoyable.

- More than half of all rapes are planned, and statistics show that assailants tend to rape more than once.
- The incestuous rapist is also a repeater. Incest is usually an established pattern in a family, with several children being victimized.
- Rape is not primarily an interracial crime. Over 90 percent of all rapes involve persons of the same race.
- Over half of all reported assaults occur in a residence, often in a victim's own home. Even more frightening is the fact that 85 percent of rapists are known to their victims. (Warning children about strangers will not necessarily keep them safe from sexual abuse.)

The following information is taken from "Crime in the United States, 1979," The Uniform Crime Report, published September 24, 1980, by the F.B.I. United States Department of Justice:
- Fifty-seven percent of those arrested for rape in 1979 were males under the age of 25, with 30 percent of those arrested in the 18–22 year age group.
- Fifty percent of those arrested for rape were white, 48 percent black, and all other races comprised the remainder.
- Forcible rape has been recognized by law enforcement as one of the most underreported of all Index crimes, primarily because of victims' fear of their assailants and their embarrassment over the incidents.
- The 1979 National Crime Survey prepared by the U.S. Bureau of the Census found that slightly over 50 percent of all rapes were reported to the police. (Other estimates put the ratio of actual rapes as high as 20 unreported for every one reported.)
- In 1979, there were 75,989 rapes reported, which is a

13.2 percent increase over 1978 and a 35 percent increase over 1975. Suburban and rural areas as well as cities indicated upsurges in the volume of forcible rape offenses.

What About Medical Help?

A person who has been sexually assaulted needs medical attention regardless of a decision to report or prosecute. The victim should be checked for internal and external bruises or bleeding, venereal diseases, and pregnancy.

Medical tests can be done for the purpose of gathering evidence, whether or not a decision has been made to prosecute. Often a victim is not ready to make that decision immediately following the assault.

Where Should the Victim Go for Help?

Hospital emergency rooms are best equipped to do the necessary tests after a rape. Many of them are now supplied with special rape kits for gathering evidence. Private physicians and health clinics are alternatives to hospital emergency rooms.

If at all possible, the victim should take a change of clothes with her to the hospital so the clothes being worn may be kept as evidence. Rape victims should *not* shower, bathe, or douche before receiving medical treatment. A rape victim should seek medical help as soon as possible, as valuable physical evidence may be lost by waiting.

What About the Legal Aspects of Rape?

Each state has its own laws concerning sexual assault. Some of the fairest, most progressive state statutes now include some or all of the following types of provisions:

- A victim need not resist the assailant. The victim need not risk being physically injured in order to prosecute.
- The testimony of a victim need not be corroborated in order to prosecute. This brings sexual assault in line with other crimes (as in robbery) where the victim's word need not be corroborated.
- The law severely restricts the admissibility of a victim's prior sexual behavior. A victim's reputation is not on trial. It is the degree of force involved which defines an assault.
- A married person can prosecute her/his spouse for sexual assault if the couple is living apart and one of them has filed for separate maintenance or divorce.
- The law extends coverage to male victims. Under the law a female or a male can be charged with criminal sexual conduct, and a female or male can prosecute.
- Attempted sexual assault can be prosecuted whether the assault involves attempted sexual penetration or sexual contact.

Some states may even provide financial reimbursement for medical expenses incurred by the victim from the assault or for salary lost due to medical problems and, in some cases, emotional problems resulting from the assault.

It may be advisable for a rape victim to investigate her own state's laws prior to prosecution. Information may be obtained from local rape crisis organizations, police, prosecuting attorneys, and private attorneys specializing in criminal law.

What About Emotional Help?

Rape is not so devastating that one cannot get over it. It is a traumatic experience that can be worked through. Many skilled people are available to provide assistance to those who need it.

Virtually every community now has a general crisis line and may have rape crisis centers as well, which can offer valuable help. Services that a rape crisis team may offer are listed below:

- Usually a team's services center around the crisis telephone line, commonly a 24-hour service.
- Team members are generally *not* professional counselors, but are trained listeners who care, understand, and know how to help. Some volunteers have been raped; many have not. Some teams have both male and female members, giving the caller the option to speak to a volunteer of either sex.
- Many teams offer in-person contact including accompanying a victim to the hospital, police station, and courtroom.
- A team may have a publicity committee or speaker's bureau, providing speakers for schools, churches, or other community groups.
- Many teams will offer information and support to family, friends, and others closely involved with the victim.
- Most teams have a confidentiality policy that is strictly observed. If you are concerned, ask your team about their policy.
- Team services may also include help for victims of obscene phone calls, sexual harassment, child molesting, incest, and other sexual crimes.
- A rape crisis team member may be able to provide information on community resources, medical, police and court procedures, and counseling alternatives if desired.
- Most rape crisis teams (except perhaps some that are funded or operated by police departments) will not pressure a victim to prosecute. They may encourage her to *report* the crime (reporting the crime does not mean a commitment to further legal action) so the option to proceed is hers later, but the main concern of the rape crisis volunteer is the welfare of

the victim. The volunteer will provide her with the information and support necessary for her to make her own decisions.

The clergy and other professional counselors may be very helpful with specific needs. Long-term counseling should be considered if a victim feels overwhelmed and unable to cope. Counseling may also be helpful if one or more feelings resulting from the rape (problems with sexuality, for example) last for a long period of time. Many rape crisis teams offer referrals for those who desire this service. A local social services department may also be of some help with referral information.

Rate your own rape crisis team for its services and your community for its resources. Are they providing the necessary help for victims who need it? Many communities have made great strides in recent years. With more and more publicity given to the crime of rape, police, medical, and legal personnel have become better aware of the victim's needs. Yet in many areas, much more needs to be done. The Christian community, with so much to offer, should be making its own impact.

What Is the Church's Response?

The church's primary response to the world is to express God's love and concern. As the body of Christ we are called to share grief and pain with those who experience it.

The pain of rape must be faced squarely and honestly by ministers and lay people. This means we must listen with understanding and not be afraid to weep with the rape victim or admonish a rape victim as the circumstances demand. Rape is a violent crime that spreads its consequences far beyond the victim. Families, friends, and children feel these consequences. We, as a church, must be sensitive and willing to bring the good news of God's grace to all circumstances where pain and alienation exist. Rape, like murder, is a crime against God and humanity. And as a crime or sin, it is something that cannot be ignored by the church. Nor can it be singled out as a special sin that somehow marks the victim for life. The victim of a rape is not someone unique or different. He or she is a person who has been a victim of man's inhumanity to man.

Rape victims are people who have experienced a violent crime. They need understanding, but they don't need continual pity or to be protected ad infinitum. May God give His people the grace and wisdom they need to give understanding and grace to those who have experienced the horror of rape.

Rev. Richard A. Jennings

What About Family and Friends? What Can We Do to Help?*

Warm, concerned, loving communication from you as family or friends is extremely important to a victim, whether or not she seeks professional counseling. A professional counselor may help, but he or she cannot replace your role in the relationship. For, more than anyone else, it is those closest to a victim who influence how she will deal with the attack.

As no situation is like any other, you will need to be sensitive to needs as they arise and recognize that there is no simple answer guaranteed to help. The following is a list of a few practical suggestions designed to ease the recovery process. Hopefully you will discover others as you offer your love and support.

---

*Portions taken from the Washington, D.C., Rape Crisis Center Newsletter, March–April, 1973.

1. Initially, most women who have been raped do not react to the sexual aspects of the crime; they react to the terror and fear that is involved. Often an immediate reaction of the woman is, "I could have been killed." Many of those around her, particularly men, may find themselves concerned with the sexual aspects of the crime. The more this preoccupation is communicated to the woman, the more likely she is to have difficulties in dealing with her own feelings. Probably the best way to understand her feelings is to remember or imagine a situation where you felt powerless and afraid (or in terror for your life).

2. It is advisable for the woman to talk about the rape; however, it is not possible to generalize about how much she should be encouraged to talk about it. Specific questions are usually callous and unkind and not appreciated by the victim. Probing for details may only worsen the problems a woman may have in dealing with the rape. Instead, questions about how she feels now and what bothers her the most are more helpful. Probably the most practical suggestion is that you communicate your own willingness to let her talk about the rape.

3. Be aware of her fears concerning you. She may be afraid that you won't believe her, that you may tell others (police, family, friends), that you may insist she relive the attack verbally, that you will be judgmental, or that she may lose control or go to pieces in front of you. Deal with these issues openly. Take a risk by bringing them up.

4. Be willing to refer to the rape directly by saying the word "rape." If you are uncomfortable with this word, the victim will feel even more ashamed.

5. Do not convey that it is not okay to cry or that she should stop. Crying is a healthy way for her to release emotions.

6. Do not preach to her or insist that her rape was God's will. She may be angry or confused about her relationship with God. Instead, encourage her to talk about these feelings.

7. Finally, because of your closeness to her, she may be more sensitive to your feelings and try to protect you. If the rape distresses you, it may be impossible for her to talk to you. If you can overcome your own need for her to talk to you and can encourage her to speak with someone whom she can trust and with whom she can feel more comfortable, you may be helping her the most. You can still offer her your warmth and love and help her with other needs.

A special note to those who know the victim but may not be especially close to her:

A blank face and silence is humiliating, as is small talk and avoiding the subject altogether. Let her know that you care about her by not being afraid to mention the rape. Not a lot needs to be said, but going on as if nothing has happened can be extremely uncomfortable for you both. Getting it out into the open will clear the air and allow your casual relationship to continue unmarred.

Stages of Adjustment

Each person going through a crisis of any kind progresses through stages of emotional adjustment. The following information is provided as a simple guideline for understanding what a rape victim may experience during her period of adjustment.

There is no time gauge to be given, as each person will deal differently within each unique situation. A victim may spend a great deal of time in one stage and only touch lightly on another. She may encounter a spiraling effect as she passes through a number of the stages over and over again, each time experiencing them with a different intensity. Anyone close to the victim may also experience these stages as he or she adjusts to the crisis of the rape as well.

1. SHOCK . . . . . Numbness.

Offering information to the victim during this stage is not helpful, as she will most likely remember very little, if anything, about what occurs during this time.

2. DENIAL . . . . . *Not me. I'm fine. This can't have happened. It's not that bad.*

Not yet able to face the severity of the crisis, the victim spends time during this stage gathering strength. The period of denial serves as a cushion for the more difficult stages of adjustment which follow.

3. ANGER . . . . . Rage, Resentment. *What did I do? Why me?*

Much of the anger may be a result of the victim's feelings of loss of strength and loss of control over her own life. The anger may be directed toward the rapist, a doctor, the police, or anyone else, including herself.

4. PLEDGE/ . . . . . Rationalization. *Let's go on as if it didn't* BARGAINING *happen. I should be finished with it by now.*

This is a further form of denial in which the victim sets up a bargain. She will not talk about the rape in exchange for not having to continue to experience the pain. In so doing, she continues to deny the emotional impact the rape has had upon her life. The rest of the bargain is that friends and relatives will also stop talking about it and pretend that it never happened.

5. DEPRESSION . . . . . Denial no longer works. *I feel so dirty . . . so worthless.*

If the victim is warned of this stage ahead of time, she may not be so thrown by it. Though a painful time for her, it is good when she reaches this stage as it shows she has begun to face the reality of the rape. As she allows the negative emotions to surface, she should be reminded that these feelings are normal and will not last forever.

She should, however, be aware of symptoms of severe depression during this stage, such as a drastic change in sleeping or eating habits, the indulging in compulsive rituals, or generalized fears completely taking over her life. Professional counseling may be advisable.

6. ACCEPTANCE . . . . . Life can go on.

When enough of the anger and depression is released, the victim enters the stage of acceptance. She may still spend time thinking and talking about the rape, but she understands and is in control of her own emotions and can now accept what has happened to her.

7. ASSIMILATION . . . . . The rape is put into perspective.

By the time the victim reaches this stage, she has realized her own self-worth and strength. She no longer needs to spend time dealing with the rape, as the total rape experience now meshes with other experiences in her life.